MIDDLE CLASS MANIFESTO

Edgar Goral

Published by Edgar Goral, contact through tatraintexas@gmail.com

ISBN 978-1-7333712-0-9 (paperback)

ISBN 978-1-7333712-1-6 (electronic book)

Library of Congress Control Number: 2019918132

Copyediting: Morgan Staggers (may be contacted through tatraintexas@gmail.com), Robert Feuerstein (robert.g.feuerstein@gmail.com), and Cindy Goral (may be contacted through tatraintexas@gmail.com)

Cover Design: Milos Jevremovic
(milos.jevremovic.srb@gmail.com)

Print Formatting: Marijo Šarić
(may be contacted through tatraintexas@gmail.com)

EDITOR'S FOREWORD

"This erosion of the middle class is happening all over the place. The opening of a wider gap between rich and poor is always accompanied by such a process."

—Susan George, English actress

"A thriving middle class is a necessary precondition for a free representative government."

—Timothy Noah, American journalist and author

In the Introduction to the *Middle Class Manifesto*, Mr. Goral states:

"In the 21st century, the middle class is disappearing. It is being systematically squeezed. Its earnings have not increased and its disposable income is being taken from them."

Those born in the mid-20th-century recall that their parents had middle-class benefits that today most don't enjoy. Their parents had pensions; today, people must map their retirement strategies with 401(k) plans. Their mothers were stay-at-home housewives; now, both parents work full-time jobs. Healthcare insurance and education costs now far exceed inflation. It's clear—the middle class is besieged from every angle imaginable.

While any number of studies support Mr. Goral's thesis, one need only look to a September 2019 *Wall Street Journal* article to verify his claim. In "Your Parents' Advice Is (Kind of) Wrong," finance reporter Julia Carpenter cites the following data:

According to the U.S. Department of Labor, "college tuition has soared 1,375% since 1978, more than four times the rate of overall inflation."

The U.S. Census Bureau observed that "median rent nationally hit a record high of $1,008 per month" in mid-2019, rising "20% faster than the overall inflation rate from 1990 to 2016."

Between 1980 and 1999, "home prices were closer to three times (median) household income." But Harvard University's Joint Center for Housing Studies found that today, "the typical U.S. home sells for more than four times the median U.S. income."

Data from the Federal Reserve indicates that "millennial households had an average net worth of about $92,000 in 2016, nearly 40% less than Gen X households (people born between 1965 and 1980) had in 2001, adjusted for inflation, and about 20% less than baby boomer households (born from 1946 to 1964) had in 1989."

Ms. Carpenter concludes, "It's time for a new playbook." Here is the *Middle Class Manifesto* - a springboard to revitalize America's middle class.

As Mr. Goral states, "Hopefully, the material herein sparks interest in further exploration on ways to bolster the middle class." I trust the *Middle Class Manifesto* will motivate you, the reader, to carefully consider how to restore and preserve the legacy of a middle-class lifestyle for your children and grandchildren.

—Morgan Staggers

EDITOR'S FOREWARD

Embedded deeply inside *Middle Class Manifesto,* after some of its innovative and fresh ideas have been fully explained, computed and justified, we find a shockingly simple two-word phrase with extraordinary meaning:

Just us.

Two one-syllable words. Six letters total. Shocking in its simplicity. Deeply profound in its importance.

The author uses 'Just Us' to describe how public policy should treat all citizens. He argues we need to get past "Us vs Them", and insert 'Just Us' as our new model. It's really Just Us here. Government needs to respect that. In a free, representative society, citizens ultimately authorize government and government needs to treat us all equally.

But the layers of meaning only start there, all directed at the basic concept of fairness. Even the words – Just Us – form an imperfect homonym for 'justice'. We all have a role in the government we get, whether we fully participate, just vote or completely stay away. We all want fairness. We want, in effect, a 'Just Us'.

What surrounds Just Us in *Middle Class Manifesto* is a package of detailed proposals covering topics we hear about frequently in this presidential election year: income inequality, tax policy, health care, maintaining a strong US labor base, supporting American farmers. What's not expected, what comes as a real surprise, are the proposed solutions.

This set of new ideas refuse to be characterized as conservative or liberal. They are not the solutions we hear during a 90-second response from a debate stage. They directly address the problems, to be sure, but the proposals come from a place we may not be familiar with. They come from a full understanding of how the problems developed through history. They come from clear-eyed interpretation of real, honest data. They come from an appreciation of how faith contributed to forming today's world.

These ideas need equal time during our public policy discussions. And we need to begin today.

—Robert Feuerstein

TABLE OF CONTENTS

INTRODUCTION

In 1848, Karl Marx wrote *The Communist Manifesto*, expressing the views and societal changes desired by The Communist Party. At the time, the concentration of wealth in the elite at the expense and impoverishment of the working class was a fundamental societal problem. The goals of the Manifesto were noble. However, its utopian vision of a perfect society was unrealistic. The idea of communal living and shared resources harkened to a time thousands of years earlier, in a simpler society with a small number of people who spent their effort, time and resources almost exclusively on agriculture. The utopian vision can no longer be achieved because that simple society cannot exist on a planet with billions of people and a complex economy.

The idea of socialism had been written about and discussed many years preceding Marx's manifesto. Modern socialism is a watered-down version of communism allowing individuals limited material possessions. In all other respects, it is in lockstep with communism.

Marx identified four classes: capitalists (rich, bourgeoisie), middle class (composed of doctors, professionals, and small business owners), working class (proletariat), and non-contributors (lumpenproletariat, composed of criminals and the chronically unemployed). Communism seeks to harness the working class to effect economic, political and social change.

The purpose of this *Middle Class Manifesto* is to address the same fundamental societal problem as *The Communist Manifesto*. Its intent: to help people understand basic economic issues in contemporary society because understanding can lead to common rational goals and realistic consensus-based solutions. The following pages also contain proposed solutions, sufficiently detailed, explaining difficult or unfamiliar concepts. In addition, this manifesto includes relevant history, most of which is no longer taught. This manifesto defines "middle class" to include Marx's middle class and working class.

In the 21st century, the middle class is disappearing. It is being systematically squeezed. Its earnings have not increased and its disposable income is being taken from them. Throughout the world, in developed and undeveloped countries alike, we hear that the gap between the rich and poor is widening. But most importantly, we hear that the middle class is disappearing into a hand-to-mouth existence with little hope for improvement. Whatever government policies and programs are in place have not been working. The time is now for new approaches and fresh ideas.

The first step is to recognize that government itself is a problem. To save the middle class, we must make fundamental changes to the government, and many will not like these changes. Government is comprised of people. People in government have a vested interest in the status quo. It takes real courage to do the right thing, especially if the right thing means distributing wealth and power to others.

The government must change the tax systems to incent corporations to pay decent wages to all employees. It CAN be done. The required modifications are included in this manifesto.

The government must also change the tax systems to incent corporations to keep the labor force employed domestically. It CAN be done. The required modifications are included in this manifesto.

The government must treat legal entities (like trusts, corporations, and organizations) no better than it treats individuals.

The government must impose controls upon itself and establish incentives to promote economic growth and prevent internal graft and corruption. The government and the private sector must grow together. This manifesto offers several suggestions, each with a meaningful measure to gauge success or failure.

If one person in society receives any government support simply because he exists, then all people in society must receive the same support. Government programs cannot use "need" as a criterion. The rationale is given in more detail in this manifesto.

Health care must be run by the private sector. This manifesto supports, both logically and mathematically, the reasons for this conclusion. Medical care has become a large section of the economy, and middle-class patients deserve effective medical care based on an intimate doctor-patient relationship, not an impersonal doctor-bureaucrat relationship.

The size of the financial sector must be reduced to provide optimal value for middle-class consumers. Competition is not working in the banking and insurance sectors. Government must impose regulations requiring participating financial arrangements, with dividends to consumers instead of profits to corporations.

Ethics are critical in any society that allows free choice. Ethics are the basis of property rights. To have ethics, you must have religion, since man can only offer "might makes right." Any member of society, including an immigrant, must have a conscience and a moral compass. All life is precious.

The *Middle Class Manifesto* contains solutions designed to promote a vibrant, healthy middle class, an essential part of an optimal society. These solutions can be adopted by any country.

WHAT CONSTITUTES A THRIVING MIDDLE CLASS?

History indicates that society does not need a thriving middle class to function. Ancient Egyptians lasted for thousands of years in a society resembling the pyramids that they spent time and resources building. A small group of rulers and priests dwelt at the top, while millions of farmers, laborers, and slaves languished at the bottom. In between, a modest class of skilled laborers and tradesmen plied their crafts along with a class of soldiers just large enough to maintain civil order.

In the last 200 years, the world has had the advantage of witnessing governmental and societal innovations. We have an idea of what works and what does not. There is an easy way to measure economic, political, or social success: Do people immigrate to your country?

A successful society is one that middle-class people living in other societies have an active desire to join. It is not simply the least despotic and oppressive option of the societies available. Middle-class people generally share certain aspirations and desires. They want a comfortable lifestyle, but also the freedom, opportunity, and ability to improve their circumstances. They want a level playing field where they can sell goods or perform services honestly, and in return receive like treatment from others. The middle class understands that society can only have a finite number of wealthy individuals, but desires to join their ranks anyway. The middle class wants to take risks and understands that risk carries a downside as well as an upside. Some members of society will fail at their endeavors and society needs to reconcile itself to that reality.

The middle class should be as large and encompassing as possible. There should be incentives for non-contributors to become members of the middle class.

CHANGES SINCE THE 1850S AND CHANGES IN THE FUTURE

The world has undergone massive changes since the publication of *The Communist Manifesto*. The one constant, though, is the concentration of wealth in the hands of a few. Changes impacting the economic vitality of the middle class are the development of new technologies, economic growth, economic diversity, the growth of non-contributors, taxation and the size of government.

TECHNOLOGY

One obvious change is the evolvement of computer technology – the digital revolution. Today governments can keep detailed information on every citizen. In particular, the government already knows or soon will know the assets and income of every domestic household. If the government wanted, it could find inconsistencies between the two, and find assets or income within the nation that have not been properly registered or reported.

In the future, the world will move to a cashless transaction system. Governments will have the capability to track every transaction, knowing every unit of income and every unit used for purchases.

ECONOMIC GROWTH – THE GROSS DOMESTIC PRODUCT

The vitality of the middle class can be determined objectively through a country's Gross Domestic Product (GDP). The year-over-year increase in GDP is a measure of economic growth.

Gross Domestic Product is a measure of how much money (or resources) a country collectively spends in a year. Two GDP-related statistics are important. The first is GDP per capita (per person), and comparisons of this statistic are made between countries. This statistic indicates the prosperity of a nation's citizens in terms of income. People tend to immigrate to a country with a high GDP per capita.

The second meaningful statistic is GDP by sector within a nation. Many economic sectors are measured: agriculture, manufacturing, mining, finance and insurance, government, health care and education, wholesale and retail trade, business services, the arts, and several others. This statistic reveals how citizens spend their time, money, and resources.

In Karl Marx's time, agriculture was the largest economic sector of GDP in Europe and America, while manufacturing was substantial and growing significantly. The rest of the world's GDP was overwhelmingly agricultural. As of 2020, only 5% of the world's GDP came from agriculture, 30% from manufacturing, and 65% from services.

The significance of this is twofold. First, in the future, there may not be enough jobs for everyone. Agriculture is essential, and manufacturing is highly desirable, but realistically we can live with much smaller finance, insurance, and entertainment sectors than we have now. Supporting the middle class means sharing the income produced from business activities more equally between owners and workers. Workers must be paid above the rate that supply and demand would dictate. There must be a set of rules (taxation) to incent owners or corporations to pay these wages.

Second, we have already seen and will continue to see changes in the relative sizes of the sectors of GDP. Developed countries now see health care approaching 15% of their GDP. Most governments in developed countries exercise a great amount of control and have a great amount of financial responsibility for health care. Politicians continuously cite burgeoning health care costs as an ongoing problem that needs further and stronger management. They do not appear to recognize that the major reason behind the growth of health care costs is the shrinkage of other sectors in today's macroeconomic society. People need jobs, and if there are no manufacturing jobs, people must find other work. Every sector (but noticeably manufacturing and agriculture) has become more efficient, requiring less labor to produce the same amount of goods.

According to socialism, the government should control the means of production. However, in the year 2020, production accounts for only 35% of GDP. Do socialists propose to control more and more of a diverse economy? Within every sector, there exist large players and small players. Government regulation, control, and enforcement are difficult, maybe even impossible, to apply to every player.

ECONOMIC DIVERSITY

The more economically diverse society is, the stronger and larger is its middle class. The rich desire objects of art, entertainment, or leisure, directly providing jobs for artists, yacht builders, hotel staff or construction workers. It also creates indirect employment for teachers, manufacturers, transporters, marketers and fuel suppliers, to name but a few. Jobs are created for skilled and unskilled labor. Workers receive specialized skills that might be useful in an entirely different industry. Innovation comes from applying the concepts learned from other industries.

Also present is the "Keeping up with the Joneses" effect. When one family brings home a new automobile or piece of technology, it creates a desire among their neighbors to do the same. This induced demand spurs growth in jobs and industry.

In a socialist society, these goods or services would not even exist. The government owns the methods of production and controls what goods or services are provided. In the interest of society, the government has the right to determine what is frivolous and what is not. In the interest of efficiency, mass production is emphasized and marketing activities are eliminated. The direct jobs and indirect jobs are never created. But people do not miss what they do not have.

The rich and the middle class often demand products and services that are not always rational. For example, many people will purchase an expensive item of clothing to use only once. It may be worn at a dance or special event. Again, jobs are created. People who earn their money have a right to spend it however they wish. These intangible goods and services, where the costs far outweigh the economic benefits, still meet a non-economic need or desire.

GROWTH OF NON-CONTRIBUTORS

Throughout history, there have been members of society who have not contributed to society. In Marx's time, non-contributors were regarded very unfavorably. No government programs were available to assist non-contributors. There were charities for the poor, but unless one could rely on family, no job meant no food. Even if one lived with extended family, he or she was expected to contribute to the household in some way.

The mantra of "From each according to his ability to pay, to each according to his needs" did not apply to the non-contributors. Communism strove to redistribute wealth from capitalists to the working class. The redistribution of wealth was never intended to include non-contributors.

Marx wrote that non-contributors were tools of the rich. Non-contributors have a vested interest in the current system, whatever system that may be. They learned how to exploit a society's behavior and programs to in essence become parasites living off the work of the middle class.

Much of the developed world no longer socially stigmatizes non-contributors to the extent found during the 19th century. For more than half a century, government programs have provided support to non-contributors. These programs were enacted with promises to end poverty. But they've had the opposite effect: They have institutionalized and perpetuated poverty. The programs created a class of people who contribute nothing but receive food, housing, medical care, and a cash stipend.

There are now generations who know no other way of life.

In 2020, about two-thirds of infants in the United States of America are born to mothers on welfare. Many public school districts provide free meals to all children because the administrative cost of keeping track of the few remaining children who do not qualify for free meals is greater than the cost to feed them.

As jobs disappear in the developed world, more people who can work and want to work are unable to find employment. Periods of unemployment for an individual worker have lengthened. Employers have shed older workers from their payrolls. Younger workers waste extra years in school, in part because jobs are scarce and in part to keep them occupied and out of the labor market.

In the future, there simply may not be enough work for everyone. Downward pressure on wages will continue, and the more generous the government support, the greater will be the number of people who find that support a viable alternative to working.

TAXES AND REDISTRIBUTION OF WEALTH

The Communist Manifesto was written at a time when there was no income tax. Government authorities had created tax systems of various kinds, usually on the sale of certain items or on the value of certain property.

In 2020, a variety of taxing schemes exist. The most significant are income tax, estate tax, value-added tax, sales tax, property tax, tariffs, and targeted taxes. These taxing systems can be modified to support the middle class.

All politicians seem to agree that some kind of redistribution of wealth is desirable, if not downright necessary. One side of the political spectrum has adopted the strategy of increasing taxes on everyone. By doing so, they have increased the taxes on the wealthy. The funds are used to increase the size of government, which are middle-class jobs, and to provide a comfortable standard of living for the most economically disadvantaged.

What they fail to recognize is the wealthy can and do adjust their economic behavior. They have the power to appropriate funds from middle-class investments and middle-class labor to make themselves economically whole. For example, the owner of a company is faced with a 2% increase in personal taxes. The owner may raise the price of the company's products, decrease employee wages, or decrease company dividends to compensate. All of these alternatives remove funds from the middle class.

The other side of the political spectrum has adopted the strategy of decreasing taxes and government spending on everyone. They believe in the trickle-down effect. They believe if the wealthy have a lower financial burden or extra funds, then they will part with every bit to bring themselves back to where they were.

What they fail to recognize is the wealthy do not adjust their economic behavior voluntarily. In this scenario, the wealthy get richer by doing nothing.

No matter which course of action is taken, the middle class is put at a disadvantage. Either their taxes are increased and disposable income decreased without economic benefit, or they wait for some wealth to trickle down into their hands.

The problem is that existing tax policy and social programs only produce these alternatives. Politicians can only move the needle on the current machine. What they need is an entirely different machine.

The following sections contain blueprints for using the tax system to improve the level and security of middle-class salaries. Also included are proposals regulating banks and insurance companies to assure middle-class consumers receive optimal value for their purchasing power.

DEFINITIONS OF ASSETS AND INCOME

When people discuss redistributing wealth, clarification of what they wish to redistribute is vitally important. Wealth can either be assets or income.

Assets are property a person already owns. Some assets are easily converted to cash or can be used as cash. They are divisible into smaller units, which when divided, equal the sum of the whole. These assets can be used to pay taxes or for consumption. Examples of convertible assets include money, loans made to other entities, stocks, and bonds.

Other assets, although valuable, cannot be converted to cash. These include works of art, jewelry, and other personal possessions as well as agricultural land and businesses. One cannot take a painting and consume part of it. Also, these assets may appreciate or depreciate over time, depending on demand for them, developments in technology, or availability of other similar assets.

In an economically diverse society, the types of assets available are also diverse. Not all assets are equal. The rich may be surrounded by objects of beauty which, if confiscated, would not feed one poor person.

Income is cash received from assets or labor. It is easily identified, measured, and redistributed.

Rich people gain wealth from other people's income. They may "manage" another person's assets for a fee. They may use another person's assets by selling him or her stock in a corporation they control. The investor buying stock receives a dividend if the corporation succeeds or loses the entire investment if the corporation fails. The corporation owner or manager returns a dividend after expenses, including his salary, to the investor if the corporation is successful, or walks away without financial consequence if the corporation fails.

Rich people gain wealth from other people's labor. A business owner hires a worker only if that worker produces revenue in excess of his wages. There may be compliance costs or other overhead that the worker will bear as a further reduction in wages. Workers compete with each other for jobs, further driving down wages. Workers with less financial need will demand less pay. Since workers usually do not consider retirement needs in their wage demands, employers only pay workers for their current financial needs. In developed countries that have laws mandating some form of taxation or set-aside for retirement, the amounts appropriated for retirement are far less than the amounts needed to provide workers with a comfortable retirement.

Rich people also gain wealth from intellectual property such as patents and copyrights. It is essential to safeguard intellectual property, no matter how substantial or trivial its value. Intellectual property can be worth a meal at a restaurant (for a book selling two copies a year) or a city block of office buildings (for fuel-efficient aviation technology). Although imitations or pirated copies of intellectual property may be easily created, people need to recognize this as theft. One should expect to receive the same punishment for stealing intellectual property as for the theft of tangible property.

Individual ownership of property is crucial to the vitality of the middle class. People will not willingly invest or work to gain property if they have no right to keep it.

Two other terms need to be defined: Production is the creation of an asset or income. Consumption is the use and elimination of the asset or income.

TAXES ON INDIVIDUAL INCOME, ASSETS, AND ESTATES

Taxes have two purposes. The first is to fund government activities. This includes defense, law enforcement, regulators and government employees, judges, building and maintenance of public roads and facilities, and interest on debt.

The second purpose is to redistribute income. Money is taken from one set of citizens and given to a different set of citizens. Income redistribution includes retirement programs, health care programs, welfare programs, and corporate incentives. No matter what the purpose, when a citizen pays taxes, he is in effect consuming the amount taken.

It is often said that "The redistribution of wealth destroys wealth." More accurate is: "The redistribution of assets destroys assets." The redistribution of income preserves income. The total income for all participants in the redistribution scheme before redistribution equals the total income for all participants after redistribution.

Taxes must be paid with money. Therefore, taxes levied against an asset force the consumption of that asset. For an asset not convertible to cash, consumption of the asset means the incremental diminution of that asset. This is particularly true if the asset is a business or a farm.

By way of illustration, let's assume that a business generates 800 units of currency a year. The government determines that the value of the business is 4,000 units, based on some method of valuation. The government imposes a tax of 15% of the asset, which is 600 units.

Table 1: Simple Example of the Effect of an Asset Tax on the Value of a Business over Time		
	Year 1	Year 2
Business Income	800	760
Taxable Value	4,000	3,800
Tax Rate	15%	15%
Tax	600	570
Living Expenses	400	400
Net Gain or Loss	(200)	(210)

The business owner has living expenses – the cost of food, clothing, utilities, and so forth. In the example above, the individual in Year 1 is forced to liquidate some of the business to live and pay taxes. The same is true for Year 2 and every subsequent year.

One problem with an asset tax: It ignores the ability to pay the tax. If the business in the above example had made only 100 units, it would still owe 600 units in tax. Another problem is the method of valuation. While the value of a portfolio of common stocks is well-defined, the value of a business is not.

The business in the example is reduced to pay the taxes. In the following year, the reduced asset generates less income.

In real life, part of a business' value is goodwill. Goodwill is the business' favorable perception by its customers. Customers value prompt service, reliability, good quality products, and appearance. They will pay extra for these services and are more likely to be repeat customers. The future expected income and margins are higher, making the business more valuable.

If part of the business were sold, or if the funds used to enhance the appearance were otherwise used to pay taxes, then not only would the tangible part of the business be reduced, but the value due to goodwill would be reduced as well. In our example, the 200 units needed to pay taxes and living expenses might reduce the value of the business by 300 units.

Property taxes are generally taxes on assets. The tax rates are usually in the range of 1% to 2% of the property's value. But taxes on assets ignore the owner's ability to pay the taxes. Sometimes an individual struggles to pay even this "nominal" amount. There are a significant amount of unpaid property taxes – not because the owners won't pay, but because the owners can't.

Another asset tax (which is used in part to redistribute income) is the estate or inheritance tax. Up until the writing of this manifesto, there is an estate tax in America which also applies to the value of farmland. The estate tax is an inheritance tax imposed at the time of death of the last surviving spouse. The tax rate can be as high as 40%.

Farms are assets. The government sets the taxable value of the land at fair market. It also includes the value of crops, livestock, buildings, and machinery. So the government sets the taxable value as high as possible. The annual gross income from farming ranges from 15% to 20% of the value of the land. After expenses, the net income from farming varies from 2% to 4% of the value of the land.

This is the national average. Smaller family farms are probably on the low end of net income as a percentage of land value. Consider then that income tax is imposed every year. Money is needed for living expenses. Every 25 to 30 years the farm has to pay an estate tax to remain in the family, regardless of the availability of funds to pay it. The sad choice for many rural families is to leave the farm.

A realistic example:

A farm has a total worth of 10 million units (or $10 million in 2020 dollars).

The net income at 2% is 200,000 units.

After an income tax of 30%, spendable and investable income is 140,000 units.

Estate Tax upon the death of the farmer is 2 million units (Note, in this example, we are treating the first 5 million units of value as exempt – in 2019 the threshold changed in the United States of America from $5 million to $11 million. According to the law, the relief is temporary).

If the farm passed to the next generation every 25 years, and the family had to set aside funds in advance to pay the estate tax, (2 million divided by 25 is 80,000 units), the family is left with a meager 60,000 units to live on. They must set aside more than half of their disposable income to retain the farm for the next generation.

This illustrates the unrelenting and unforgiving devastation of family farms by the government through its tax policies. Viewed from an investor's perspective, very few investors would apply funds where the expected rate of return is only 2%-4%, where there is a relatively high probability of losing a substantial amount of money (crop failure), and where the tax treatment is more onerous than other investments.

The disincentives to farm in America have come from financial pressure on existing farms and the discouragement of expansion or new entrants to farming. The cost to borrow is 6%-10% of the loan. If the return on the investment from loan proceeds is only 2%-4%, no one would be willing to borrow money to invest in or expand an existing farm.

CORPORATIONS, NON-PROFITS, AND TRUSTS

Corporations are legal entities that exist because governments allow them. People exist no matter what the form of government. This is not true for corporations. They are defined, licensed, and taxed by governments. Also, governments recognize the existence of nonprofit corporations and trusts. Again, these entities operate according to rules set by the governments. These rules may or may not be consistent between categories of legal entities, and may or may not even be consistent within a certain category. Governments have the right to set whatever rules they want as long as the rules are published and enforced fairly.

Churches exist because they fill a need in society. In addition to providing spiritual guidance and assistance, most churches perform some kind of public charity. Many distribute food or clothing to the needy. They have had a unique tax status because governments realized that churches exist independently from government, and taxing them would be extraordinarily unpopular. Other non-profit corporations have attained the same tax treatment as churches. But this does not have to be. Non-profit corporations are fundamentally different from churches. Non-profit corporations exist because governments define, license, and can tax them. Because these entities owe their existence to the government, they should pay an appropriate tax to the government.

Trusts are set up by wealthy individuals, who then draw on the trust when needed. Once a wealthy individual dies, his or her heirs manage and draw from funds in the trust, either directly or through a foundation. In many jurisdictions, trusts live forever. Other jurisdictions impose an expiration date on certain trusts which potentially could allow them to operate for several lifetimes. Trusts, like corporations, owe their existence to the government. In America, trusts are subject to income tax rules similar to individuals. However, they are not subject to inheritance taxes because they never technically die.

SOLUTION: TAXATION OF TRUSTS

Trusts are created for a variety of reasons – some of which serve an important purpose. A valid reason for setting up a trust is when an heir is not yet an adult and needs an inheritance preserved until adulthood is reached. A less noble reason is to transfer the benefits of assets without the technical legal ownership of those assets to a person receiving a government stipend based on need. Some types of trusts are set up for the express purpose of avoiding the estate tax. These trusts have limited lifespans and must be reestablished every generation or two.

Many wealthy people set up a charitable trust in conjunction with a non-profit "foundation." Assets are managed in the trust. A transfer of funds is made periodically from the trust to the foundation. It is then the foundation's responsibility to disburse those funds. This arrangement is set up ostensibly to provide ongoing charitable activities long after the death of the founder. The founder's heirs are expected to manage the trust and foundation as long as funds exist, which could in theory be forever.

Why use trusts and foundations to fund charitable activities? Wealthy people could easily support charitable work without trusts. Part of the answer lies in the administrative expenses associated with operating trusts and foundations.

Most trusts are mechanisms used to pass immense estates to heirs without paying any estate taxes. The heirs receive an ongoing income from the trust's investments. The income may be paid directly or through the associated non-profit foundation. The heirs are the board of directors and the officers of the trust and foundation, receiving salaries from the trust.

The following is a simple example of how trusts operate and how trusts are taxed. "Administrative expenses" incurred by the trust are actually inheritance proceeds paid to heirs. Trusts pay income taxes on their investment earnings less administrative expenses. Recipients of the trust's administrative expenses pay individual taxes on those amounts.

In the simple example, wealthy person Gen1 has amassed 10 million units at the time of his death. He has one heir – Gen2. We will assume that the estate tax rate is 40% and all assets earn a 5% return.

Without a trust, Gen2 inherits 6 million units (10 million estate less 4 million in estate tax). These 6 million units provide an income of 300,000 units (6 million times 5%).

If Gen1 sets up a trust with the full 10 million units, then upon his death there is no estate tax. Gen2 is the president of the trust. The trust earns 500,000 units and provides charity of 5,000 units. This leaves 495,000 units for administrative expenses. Gen2 is better off financially under a trust arrangement than simply inheriting the estate.

Gen2 can grow the trust. He may choose to take only 300,000 units, pay the income tax (assume a rate of 35%) on the remaining 195,000 units, and grow the trust by the remaining 126,750 units. The following year, the trust earns 506,337 units.

Assume that the trust pays 5,000 units to charity and 495,000 units to Gen2 every year for 25 years. Also assume that after 25 years, Gen2 dies and has one heir, Gen3. Without a trust, Gen3 would inherit 3.6 million units after estate taxes which provides an income of 180,000 units per year. With the trust, Gen3 receives 495,000 units per year.

The taxation of trusts should follow the taxation of individuals. Income taxes on trusts should not be lower than income taxes on individuals. Trusts should not escape the estate tax.

The primary purpose of the estate tax is to confiscate the assets of those individuals having assets above a certain threshold. It is designed to reduce asset disparity within a society. It was never intended to have loopholes, allowing avoidance by creating the right documents.

Several changes in the tax law could make estate taxes fairer.

The most desirable solution by far is to abolish all estate taxes. The reasons were discussed earlier. An asset tax diminishes the wealth of a society. The estate tax encourages the wealthy to over-accumulate and to take as much wealth from others as they can since eventually, they (their heirs) will have to part with about half of it.

If society insists on an estate tax on individuals, then it must impose the estate tax on all other legal entities as consistently as possible.

First, the estate tax should be imposed on the entire estate whenever a trust is established. For example, an individual whose net worth is 10 million units establishes a trust worth only 10 thousand units for a relative. The event triggers payment of the estate tax, calculated on the entire 10 million. In real life, the estate tax is imposed at the moment when assets are transferred from the deceased to his or her heirs. When a trust is established, assets are also deemed transferred. So the timing of the estate tax imposition is consistent with the passing of assets. Imposing the estate tax on the entire estate is needed to prevent tax avoidance by forming 100 little trusts, each below the estate tax threshold.

Second, once a trust is established, then the estate tax should be imposed on that trust every twenty years. This fully mimics the tax treatment for individuals. Individuals pass away, leaving their estates to heirs every twenty to fifty years. Trusts should do the same.

The imposition of the recurring twenty-year estate tax on trusts would lead to reexamining the question of why trusts exist, and would probably result in the abolishment of estate taxes since estate taxes would then apply to the rich in every instance.

The recurring twenty-year estate tax should apply to corporations, partnerships, non-profit organizations, and any other legal entity with an unlimited lifespan, or lifespan greater than twenty years. This would be consistent with the principle of taxing legal entities no more favorably than individuals.

Third, the tax rate for trusts should be higher than the tax rate for individuals. This principle applies to each type of tax, whether it is income, estate, VAT or property tax. Currently, in the United States of America, the income tax rates are the same. Trusts must provide value over and above individual savings or investment accounts. The government should share in that value. Also, by distributing all the income to the beneficiary every year, the trust would incur no income tax, so the rate is irrelevant.

The tax rate for corporations and other legal entities should also be higher than the rate imposed on individuals. The wealthy have huge stakes in corporations. The corporate income tax rate is essentially the income tax rate on the wealthy. Corporations can shoulder an estate tax much easier than an individual can. Much like the example given earlier in this manifesto on the farm finances, the corporation would set aside funds every year equal to one-twentieth of the estimated estate tax. The value of most corporations is easy to determine. It is the average price per share of stock over some historical period times the outstanding number of shares.

A related issue is estate taxes on widows (and widowers). Many countries do not impose an estate tax on the surviving spouse. In theory, successive marriage has the same effect as creating an estate tax-exempt trust. For example, Gen1 and Wid1 are married. Upon Gen1's death, Wid1 inherits everything tax-free. Wid1 then marries an 18-year-old, then dies one year later. The 18-year-old gets the estate of Gen1 tax-free. This situation, where the system can be gamed, is another reason for the abolishment of estate taxes.

Again, if society insists on taxing estates, then the surviving spouse exemption should end if and when the survivor remarries. Thereupon the estate tax is imposed on the new couple.

SOLUTION: CHANGES TO THE CORPORATE INCOME TAX – DYNAMIC TAX RATE AND THE FAIR DISTRIBUTION TAX

Corporations pay an income tax based on their earnings. Earnings are simply revenue less expenses (cost of materials and administration) less other deductions (depreciation). The tax rate is usually the same for all corporations. Any favorable tax treatment usually shows up in other deductions.

The corporate income tax was patterned after individual income tax, except most corporate expenses were deductible from revenue while most individual personal expenses were not. The purpose of the corporate income tax was the same as the individual tax – to raise money for the government.

Corporations employ a significant percentage of the middle class. As previously noted, corporations are authorized by the government, and the government can make any tax rule it wishes.

Income inequality truly exists worldwide, and it affects the middle class directly. In 2020 and beyond, the tax code needs to be changed to encourage corporations to pay workers higher wages than simple supply and demand would dictate. The government can give corporations the choice – either pay your workers more equitably or pay higher taxes to the government and it will dole the money out to your workers and any other members of society according to their perceived needs.

The change in the tax code addresses income inequality. The government would examine not only the total amount of corporate expenditures but the distribution of those expenditures as well. The more even the distribution, the lower the income tax. Corporations are controlled by the very rich. They need workers, including private contractors, to function.

The underlying financial information and required technology already exist to implement the necessary changes to the corporate income tax methodology. This manifesto contains the blueprint to encourage more generous treatment of middle-class employees by corporations through the corporate tax system. It can be done! The new corporate income tax includes a fair distribution tax, which is determined by how equitably income is distributed within the corporation.

One fundamental change to corporate income tax would be the introduction of the dynamic tax rate. Here is how it works: The income tax rate depends on the percentage of taxable income and salary including benefits given to the top ten percent of corporate income recipients (corporate executives, major shareholders, major independent contractors). The more even the pay structure is among all participants (employees and investors), the lower the income tax rate. By way of a simple example, there are two corporations. Each has 10 employees. No dividends are paid to shareholders.

Management and employees receive the following compensation:

Table 2: Simple Example showing Salary of Employees sorted by Amount of Salary

Employee	Company #1 Salary	Company #2 Salary
1	100	550
2	100	50
3	100	50
4	100	50
5	100	50
6	100	50
7	100	50
8	100	50
9	100	50
10	100	50
Total	1,000	1,000

The following table shows company earnings, taxes, and the increase in surplus under a dynamic tax system. An explanation of each line within the table is shown immediately below:

The Corporate Income Tax Rate is 35%. The Corporate Income Tax is the Corporate Income Tax Rate multiplied by the Earnings Before Income Tax.

We add a new adjustment called the "Standard Management Share." This is defined as the nationally acceptable percentage of salary and benefits of the top 10% to the total within the corporation. This percentage may vary inversely with the size of the corporation. In our simple example, we will set the Standard Management Share to 25%.

The "Company Management Share" has the same meaning as the Standard Management Share, but is based on the specific corporation being taxed. In our example, Company #1's Company Management Share is 100/1,000 = 0.1 or 10%. Company #2's is 550/1,000 = 0.55 or 55%.

The "Management Share Adjustment" is the Company Management Share less the Standard Management Share. There would be a multiplier applied to this difference. The formula would be (CMS-SMS) X multiplier. In our example, the multiplier is 1.0. Again, the multiplier may vary by company size. Its purpose is to give the needed leverage in determining tax rates and has analogs throughout the tax codes.

The "Fair Distribution Tax" is the Management Share Adjustment multiplied by the sum of Earnings Before Income Tax and Salary, Benefits, and Dividends.

Finally, the Total Corporate Tax is the sum of the Corporate Income Tax and the Fair Distribution Tax.

The Increase in Company Surplus is the Earnings Before Income Tax less Total Corporate Tax.

Let's assume that the corporations had a good year, earning 3,000 units before income taxes.

Table 3: Simple Example showing Dynamic Tax System's Effects on Company Earnings, Taxes, and Increase in Surplus when Companies had a Profitable Year		
	Company #1	Company #2
Earnings Before Income Tax	3,000	3,000
Corporate Income Tax Rate	35%	35%
Corporate Income Tax	1,050	1,050
Salary, Benefits, Dividends	1,000	1,000
Standard Management Share	25%	25%
Company Management Share	10%	55%
Management Share Adjustment	(15%)	30%
Fair Distribution Tax	(600)	1,200
Total Corporate Tax	450	2,250
Increase in Company Surplus	2,550	750

This example illustrates several points:

First and most importantly, the corporation has an incentive to pay its employees higher wages. Management has a choice: pay their employees more or pay higher taxes. Higher taxes mean the government decides how to spend the extra revenue. It could increase spending on social programs, which may or may not offer some value to the middle class.

Second, a company paying more equitable wages gets to increase its surplus and has funds needed for growth. This supports a more viable and competitive company.

Third, Company #2's tax burden is high enough for the government to give every employee an extra 50 units, putting them at the same level as Company #1. The extra taxes come at the sacrifice of company surplus.

For Company #1 having a good year, the impact of doubling or tripling everyone's salary is shown in the following table. In this example, wages are completely level; only the magnitude has changed.

Table 4: Simple Example showing the Effects of Doubling and Tripling of Every Employee's Salary on Company Earnings, Taxes, and Increase in Surplus under a Dynamic Tax System		
	Company #1, pay everyone 200	Company #1, pay everyone 300
Earnings Before Income Tax	2,000	1,000
Corporate Income Tax Rate	35%	35%
Corporate Income Tax	700	350
Salary, Benefits, Dividends	2,000	3,000
Standard Management Share	25%	25%
Company Management Share	10%	10%
Management Share Adjustment	(15%)	(15%)
Fair Distribution Tax	(600)	(600)
Total Corporate Tax	100	(250)
Increase in Company Surplus	1,900	1,250

This example helps to demonstrate:

First, the increase in pay is a decrease to earnings.

Second, a company can afford to hand out bonuses to everyone in a good year – both to employees and shareholders. The company still experiences an increase in company surplus. Should salaries be tripled, the company makes money and gets a tax refund. The company is rewarded for paying its workers on par with management.

Third, a company with a flatter pay structure can reward everyone more and still have a higher increase in surplus than a company in which management hoards as much earnings as possible.

Now let's assume the corporations had a bad year, earning 300 units before income taxes.

Table 5: Simple Example showing Dynamic Tax System's Effects on Company Earnings, Taxes, and Increase in Surplus when Companies had an Unprofitable Year		
	Company #1	Company #2
Earnings Before Income Tax	300	300
Corporate Income Tax Rate	35%	35%
Corporate Income Tax	105	105
Salary, Benefits, Dividends	1,000	1,000
Standard Management Share	25%	25%
Company Management Share	10%	55%
Management Share Adjustment	(15%)	30%
Fair Distribution Tax	(195)	390
Total Corporate Tax	(90)	495
Increase in Company Surplus	390	(195)

This example illustrates:

First, this represents the situation where management is giving poor direction. For Company #2, while the company suffers, management prospers. Management's salary exceeds company earnings.

Second, because management takes too large of a share of total salary in Company #2, the tax liability is greater than corporate earnings before income tax, and company surplus will be applied to taxes. This means that Company #2 will shrink. It must shed some of its assets. Management, unfortunately, will have a smaller cow to milk next year.

Third, because of the Fair Distribution Tax, Company #1 receives a small refund. It can grow slightly, but no bonuses are available for this year.

In summary, a corporate income tax that includes a Fair Distribution Tax will incent corporations to pay workers and shareholders a larger percentage of earnings. Companies that share more will grow more. Employees will have a greater incentive to work harder. Not only will they receive more money, but the company provides them a brighter future with better job security.

Society is giving private enterprise an incentive to reward middle-class workers. The reward comes from both wealthy management and successful corporations. Society overlays a communistic tax program atop a capitalistic economic system. There are private ownership and operation of business but the business is run for the benefit of all involved. The "us versus them" mindset is lessened.

This is necessarily a simple but powerful example. In real life, the definition of what constitutes a person for the purpose of corporate income tax is needed. Similar wording already exists in the tax code for other purposes. Some employees do not work a full year. Some assignments or functions are given to private contractors. A definition of what constitutes a shareholder for the Fair Distribution Tax is also needed. The increase in the value of golden parachutes or other management incentives also needs to be recognized and quantified.

But the first step is understanding the concept of a fair distribution tax and realizing that it can be used to alleviate income inequality.

SOLUTION: THE FAIR DISTRIBUTION TAX AND EXPORTING JOBS TO OTHER COUNTRIES

Manufacturing jobs have steadily relocated from the developed world to the underdeveloped world. Manufacturing a product in a foreign country is cheaper since the cost of foreign labor plus the cost of transportation is less than the cost of domestic labor. Foreign labor may be one-tenth of the cost of domestic labor. The cost of foreign compliance and foreign taxation could also be significantly less.

As telecommuting and home employment become more widespread in technology and "office" sectors, jobs will be filled in those countries where qualified labor is cheapest. Current tax law encourages corporations to move as much labor as possible to foreign countries.

A simple example of corporate earnings under current tax law is shown below. The example describes a company where the only corporate expense is labor and the corporation has decided to move its labor to a foreign country where the cost of labor is half the cost of domestic labor.

Table 6: Simple Example showing the Effects on Company Earnings, Taxes, and Increase in Surplus under Current Tax Law when a Company Moves Operations to a Foreign Country

	Company Maintains Domestic Operations	Company Moves Operations to Foreign Country
Revenues	1,000	1,000
Domestic Labor Expense	800	0
Foreign Labor Expense	0	400
Earnings Before Income Tax	200	600
Corporate Income Tax Rate	35%	35%
Corporate Income Tax	70	210
Increase in Company Surplus	130	390

The example shows the corporation is better off financially by reducing expenses. The winners are the wealthy corporate owners and workers in other countries. The loser is the domestic middle class.

But how is government revenue affected? The government receives more revenue from the corporation but loses the tax revenue and economic activity from the displaced middle-class jobs. The table below illustrates this point:

Table 7: Simple Example comparing Total Tax Revenues from the Corporation and its Employees when a Company Moves Operations to a Foreign Country

	Company Maintains Domestic Operations	Company Moves Operations to Foreign Country
Domestic Labor Expense	800	0
Individual Tax Rate	20%	20%
Individual Tax Revenue	160	0
Corporate Income Tax Revenue	70	210
Total Tax Revenues	230	210

This simple example illustrates how the government can be worse off when corporate jobs are moved to a foreign country. Management, labor, and government have divergent financial incentives under current corporate tax law. As long as current tax laws remain, jobs will continue migrating to lower-wage nations.

The Fair Distribution Tax and modification of the corporate income tax can reverse the incentive to export jobs. The Fair Distribution Tax is a calculation based on all employees and shareholders worldwide. Again, a simple example illustrates the use of the Fair Distribution Tax on company earnings, taxes, and growth when a company decides to send jobs to another country with cheaper labor.

When jobs move out of the country, both domestic income tax revenue and funds for domestic purchasing are reduced. 100 units paid to a foreign employee is not as valuable to a country as 100 units paid to a domestic employee. Therefore, any tax calculation should recognize the relatively low value of foreign workers to a country.

Two viable ways to incorporate labor performed in another country into the corporate income tax are shown in the following examples. Each way has two sub-alternatives, whether the cost of foreign labor is a deductible business expense or not.

In these examples, we start with the corporations #1 and #2 from the Solution: Changes to the Corporate Income Tax – Dynamic Tax Rate and the Fair Distribution Tax section of this manifesto. Now one change is made – each company has moved 40% of its workforce to another country where the cost of labor is half of its current labor costs. The savings in labor is reflected as higher earnings.

Management and employees receive the following revised compensation:

Table 8: Simple Example showing Salary of Employees sorted by Amount of Salary

Employee	Company #1 Salary	Company #2 Salary
1	100	550
2	100	50
3	100	50
4	100	50
5	100	50
6	100	50
7	50	25
8	50	25
9	50	25
10	50	25
Total	800	900

If we calculate the new Company Management Share giving full recognition to foreign labor, then the Company Management Share for Company #1 is 100/800 = 0.125 or 12.5%. Company #2's is 550/900 = 0.6111 or 61.11%. This represents the situation where foreign labor is neither encouraged nor discouraged. Only the impact of wage reduction is demonstrated.

Under the scenario where the corporations had a good year:

Table 9: Simple Example showing the Effects of Moving a Portion of Operations to a Foreign Country on Company Earnings, Taxes, and Increase in Surplus under a Dynamic Tax System when Companies had a Profitable Year		
	Company #1	Company #2
Earnings Before Income Tax	3,200	3,100
Corporate Income Tax Rate	35%	35%
Corporate Income Tax	1,120	1,085
Salary, Benefits, Dividends	800	900
Standard Management Share	25%	25%
Company Management Share	12.5%	61.11%
Management Share Adjustment	(12.5%)	36.11%
Fair Distribution Tax	(500)	1,444.44
Total Corporate Tax	620	2,529.44
Increase in Company Surplus	2,580	570.56

Under the scenario where the corporations had a bad year:

Table 10: Simple Example showing the Effects of Moving a Portion of Operations to a Foreign Country on Company Earnings, Taxes, and Increase in Surplus under a Dynamic Tax System when Companies had an Unprofitable Year		
	Company #1	Company #2
Earnings Before Income Tax	500	400
Corporate Income Tax Rate	35%	35%
Corporate Income Tax	175	140
Salary, Benefits, Dividends	800	900
Standard Management Share	25%	25%
Company Management Share	12.5%	61.11%
Management Share Adjustment	(12.5%)	36.11%
Fair Distribution Tax	(162.5)	469.44
Total Corporate Tax	(12.5)	609.44
Increase in Company Surplus	487.5	(209.44)

The two tables above are included to show the starting points of a taxation system that includes a corporate Fair Distribution Tax. Foreign labor is treated on the same basis as domestic labor. Showing these starting points is necessary because the cost of labor, and therefore the Earnings Before Income Tax, have changed from the baselines presented in the Solution: Changes to the Corporate Income Tax – Dynamic Tax Rate and the Fair Distribution Tax section.

The first way to adjust corporate income tax for foreign labor is to recognize foreign labor in the Fair Distribution Tax component at a fraction of its cost. The fraction may be any number less than one, and could even be negative. Then, a second adjustment is the actual allowance or disallowance of foreign labor as a valid business expense deduction.

In the following simple example, 10% of foreign labor is recognized in the Fair Distribution Tax.

The "Recognized Salary" calculation is shown below:

Table 11: Simple Example showing Actual Salary and Recognized Salary for Tax Purposes sorted by Amount of Salary

Employee	Company #1 Actual Salary	Company #1 Recognized Salary	Company #2 Actual Salary	Company #2 Recognized Salary
1 Domestic	100	100	550	550
2 Domestic	100	100	50	50
3 Domestic	100	100	50	50
4 Domestic	100	100	50	50
5 Domestic	100	100	50	50
6 Domestic	100	100	50	50
7 Foreign	50	5	25	2.5
8 Foreign	50	5	25	2.5
9 Foreign	50	5	25	2.5
10 Foreign	50	5	25	2.5
Total	800	620	900	810
Company Management Share		100/620 = 16.13%		550/810 = 67.90%

If foreign labor is an allowable business deduction, the income statements, taxes, and increases in company surplus are as follows:

Under the scenario where the corporations had a good year:

Table 12: Simple Example showing the Effects of Recognized Salary on Company Earnings, Taxes, and Increase in Surplus under a Dynamic Tax System for Companies with Foreign Operations when Companies had a Profitable Year and Foreign Salary is a Deductible Expense		
	Company #1	Company #2
Earnings Before Income Tax	3,200	3,100
Corporate Income Tax Rate	35%	35%
Corporate Income Tax	1,120	1,085
Salary, Benefits, Dividends	800	900
Standard Management Share	25%	25%
Company Management Share	16.13%	67.90%
Management Share Adjustment	(8.87%)	42.90%
Fair Distribution Tax	(354.84)	1,716.05
Total Corporate Tax	765.16	2,801.05
Increase in Company Surplus	2,434.84	298.95

Under the scenario where the corporations had a bad year:

Table 13: Simple Example showing the Effects of Recognized Salary on Company Earnings, Taxes, and Increase in Surplus under a Dynamic Tax System for Companies with Foreign Operations when Companies had an Unprofitable Year and Foreign Salary is a Deductible Expense		
	Company #1	Company #2
Earnings Before Income Tax	500	400
Corporate Income Tax Rate	35%	35%
Corporate Income Tax	175	140
Salary, Benefits, Dividends	800	900
Standard Management Share	25%	25%
Company Management Share	16.13%	67.90%
Management Share Adjustment	(8.87%)	42.90%
Fair Distribution Tax	(115.32)	557.72
Total Corporate Tax	59.68	697.72
Increase in Company Surplus	440.32	(297.72)

If foreign labor is not an allowable business deduction, the income statements, taxes, and increases in company surplus are as follows:

Under the scenario where the corporations had a good year:

Table 14: Simple Example showing the Effects of Recognized Salary on Company Earnings, Taxes, and Increase in Surplus under a Dynamic Tax System for Companies with Foreign Operations when Companies had a Profitable Year and Foreign Salary is NOT a Deductible Expense		
	Company #1	Company #2
Earnings Before Income Tax	3,400	3,200
Corporate Income Tax Rate	35%	35%
Corporate Income Tax	1,190	1,120
Salary, Benefits, Dividends	800	900
Standard Management Share	25%	25%
Company Management Share	16.13%	67.90%
Management Share Adjustment	(8.87%)	42.90%
Fair Distribution Tax	(372.58)	1,758.95
Total Corporate Tax	817.42	2,878.95
Non-Deductible Salaries	200	100
Increase in Company Surplus	2,382.58	221.05

Under the scenario where the corporations had a bad year:

Table 15: Simple Example showing the Effects of Recognized Salary on Company Earnings, Taxes, and Increase in Surplus under a Dynamic Tax System for Companies with Foreign Operations when Companies had an Unprofitable Year and Foreign Salary is NOT a Deductible Expense		
	Company #1	Company #2
Earnings Before Income Tax	700	500
Corporate Income Tax Rate	35%	35%
Corporate Income Tax	245	175
Salary, Benefits, Dividends	800	900
Standard Management Share	25%	25%
Company Management Share	16.13%	67.90%
Management Share Adjustment	(8.87%)	42.90%
Fair Distribution Tax	(133.06)	600.62
Total Corporate Tax	111.94	775.62
Non-Deductible Salaries	200	100
Increase in Company Surplus	388.06	(375.62)

The second way to adjust corporate income tax for foreign labor is to include foreign labor with the top 10% tier in the Fair Distribution Tax component. Then, as in the first way to adjust the corporate income tax for foreign labor, a second step is the allowance or disallowance of foreign labor as a valid business expense deduction.

The "Tier-Reassigned Salary" calculation is shown below:

Table 16: Simple Example showing Actual Salary and Tier-Reassigned Salary for Tax Purposes sorted by Amount of Salary

Employee	Company #1 Actual Salary	Company #1 Tier Reassignment	Company #2 Actual Salary	Company #2 Tier Reassignment
1 High plus Foreign	100	300	550	650
2 Domestic	100	100	50	50
3 Domestic	100	100	50	50
4 Domestic	100	100	50	50
5 Domestic	100	100	50	50
6 Domestic	100	100	50	50
7 Foreign	50		25	
8 Foreign	50		25	
9 Foreign	50		25	
10 Foreign	50		25	
Total	800	800	900	900
Company Management Share		300/800 = 37.50%		650/900 = 72.22%

If foreign labor is an allowable business deduction, the income statements, taxes, and increases in company surplus are as follows:

Under the scenario where the corporations had a good year:

Table 17: Simple Example showing the Effects of Tier-Reassigned Salary on Company Earnings, Taxes, and Increase in Surplus under a Dynamic Tax System for Companies with Foreign Operations when Companies had a Profitable Year and Foreign Salary is a Deductible Expense

	Company #1	Company #2
Earnings Before Income Tax	3,200	3,100
Corporate Income Tax Rate	35%	35%
Corporate Income Tax	1,120	1,085
Salary, Benefits, Dividends	800	900
Standard Management Share	25%	25%
Company Management Share	37.50%	72.22%
Management Share Adjustment	12.50%	47.22%
Fair Distribution Tax	500.00	1,888.89
Total Corporate Tax	1.620.00	2,973.89
Increase in Company Surplus	1,580.00	126.11

Under the scenario where the corporations had a bad year:

Table 18: Simple Example showing the Effects of Tier-Reassigned Salary on Company Earnings, Taxes, and Increase in Surplus under a Dynamic Tax System for Companies with Foreign Operations when Companies had an Unprofitable Year and Foreign Salary is a Deductible Expense		
	Company #1	Company #2
Earnings Before Income Tax	500	400
Corporate Income Tax Rate	35%	35%
Corporate Income Tax	175	140
Salary, Benefits, Dividends	800	900
Standard Management Share	25%	25%
Company Management Share	37.50%	72.22%
Management Share Adjustment	12.50%	47.22%
Fair Distribution Tax	162.50	613.89
Total Corporate Tax	337.50	753.89
Increase in Company Surplus	162.50	(353.89)

If foreign labor is not an allowable business deduction, the income statements, taxes, and increases in company surplus are as follows:

Under the scenario where the corporations had a good year:

Table 19: Simple Example showing the Effects of Tier-Reassigned Salary on Company Earnings, Taxes, and Increase in Surplus under a Dynamic Tax System for Companies with Foreign Operations when Companies had a Profitable Year and Foreign Salary is NOT a Deductible Expense		
	Company #1	Company #2
Earnings Before Income Tax	3,400	3,200
Corporate Income Tax Rate	35%	35%
Corporate Income Tax	1,190	1,120
Salary, Benefits, Dividends	800	900
Standard Management Share	25%	25%
Company Management Share	37.50%	72.22%
Management Share Adjustment	12.50%	47.22%
Fair Distribution Tax	525.00	1,936.11
Total Corporate Tax	1,715.00	3,056.11
Non-Deductible Salaries	200	100
Increase in Company Surplus	1,485.00	43.89

Under the scenario where the corporations had a bad year:

Table 20: Simple Example showing the Effects of Tier-Reassigned Salary on Company Earnings, Taxes, and Increase in Surplus under a Dynamic Tax System for Companies with Foreign Operations when Companies had an Unprofitable Year and Foreign Salary is NOT a Deductible Expense		
	Company #1	Company #2
Earnings Before Income Tax	700	500
Corporate Income Tax Rate	35%	35%
Corporate Income Tax	245	175
Salary, Benefits, Dividends	800	900
Standard Management Share	25%	25%
Company Management Share	37.50%	72.22%
Management Share Adjustment	12.50%	47.22%
Fair Distribution Tax	187.50	661.11
Total Corporate Tax	432.50	836.11
Non-Deductible Salaries	200	100
Increase in Company Surplus	67.50	(436.11)

Below is a summary of the impact on company surplus of various tax treatments when companies move jobs to a foreign country. The entries in this table come from the Increase in Company Surplus lines from the scenario tables in this section of the manifesto.

Table 21: Summary of the Increase in Company Surplus from Alternate Methodologies of Treating the Cost of Foreign Labor under the Dynamic Tax System				
	Company #1, Good Year	Company #2, Good Year	Company #1, Bad Year	Company #2, Bad Year
Jobs Retained by Domestic Employees	2,550	750	390	(195)
Jobs Transferred, Tax Unchanged	2,580	571	488	(209)
Jobs Transferred, Fair Distribution Tax based on fraction of foreign salary, which is a deductible business expense	2,435	299	440	(298)
Jobs Transferred, Fair Distribution Tax based on fraction of foreign salary, which is NOT a deductible business expense	2,383	221	388	(376)
Jobs Transferred, Fair Distribution Tax based on tier reassignment of foreign salary, which is a deductible business expense	1,580	126	163	(354)
Jobs Transferred, Fair Distribution Tax based on tier reassignment of foreign salary, which is NOT a deductible business expense	1,485	44	68	(436)

Below is a comparison of each method of tax treatment to retaining jobs domestically. The entries in this table come from the prior table. Line 3 in this table is line 3 from the prior table less line 1 from the prior table. A positive number means that the company is financially better off when it moves jobs to a foreign country.

Table 22: Impact to Company Surplus of Moving Jobs to a Foreign Country under Alternative Salary Recognition Rules in the Dynamic Tax System

	Company #1, Good Year	Company #2, Good Year	Company #1, Bad Year	Company #2, Bad Year
Jobs Retained by Domestic Employees	0	0	0	0
Jobs Transferred, Tax Unchanged	30	(179)	98	(14)
Jobs Transferred, Fair Distribution Tax based on fraction of foreign salary, which is a deductible business expense	(115)	(451)	50	(103)
Jobs Transferred, Fair Distribution Tax based on fraction of foreign salary, which is NOT a deductible business expense	(167)	(529)	(2)	(181)
Jobs Transferred, Fair Distribution Tax based on tier reassignment of foreign salary, which is a deductible business expense	(970)	(624)	(227)	(159)
Jobs Transferred, Fair Distribution Tax based on tier reassignment of foreign salary, which is NOT a deductible business expense	(1,065)	(706)	(322)	(241)

These simple examples illustrate the following:

First, there IS a way to encourage domestic companies to promote domestic employment through the corporate income tax system. One should keep in mind that corporations exist from governmental authority, and the government can set any tax rule it likes on corporations.

Second, scenarios exist when it makes economic sense to move labor abroad. Successful companies wishing to reward management are generally better off retaining labor domestically.

Third, retaining labor domestically promotes the middle class and therefore the domestic economy. Domestic labor purchases local goods and services.

Fourth, the taxation of a multinational company involves gathering financial information from all countries in which it operates. In the calculation of the Company Management Share, in the first way to incorporate foreign labor, any foreign salaries falling in the top 10% should not be decremented, unlike foreign salaries in the bottom 90%.

Fifth, the taxation of a multinational company whose headquarters and a majority of its operations are in other countries is not discussed in detail. In this case, the Company Management Share is a formula based on the worldwide salary distribution, the amount and percentage of company business and salaries paid domestically, and any inherent biases to encourage or discourage certain business, or to adjust for unfair foreign government support. There would be retaliatory taxes as well.

Sixth, the taxation of a multinational company is partly based on public policy. Much depends on the level of foreign capital society wants entering the home country and the level of capital society will allow to leave through corporate profits.

Seventh, financial modeling which includes income tax adjustments can and should be used to set reasonable tariffs that create a level playing field for every industry. Products produced in foreign countries by foreign corporations are outside of the domestic tax system. However, the government can recalculate the price of a commodity, substituting domestic labor, domestic taxes, and domestic overhead like reasonable rent. Using tariffs to encourage the retention and development of domestic industries is an established and acceptable tool.

SOLUTION: TAXATION OF NON-PROFITS AND PASS-THROUGH CHARITIES

A pass-through charity is a marketing organization licensed as a non-profit corporation or organization. It collects money for a "worthy cause" and distributes a small percentage of collections to that cause. The worthy cause may be an actual charity or may perform research or medical treatment.

These pass-through charities are authorized by government licensure and classified as non-profit because technically they somehow distribute all funds collected, either to programs associated with their worthy cause or to their salaries and marketing expenses, but there are no "profits." These organizations are distinct from churches in that churches can and would exist in the absence of government. Also, churches are the final recipients of funds donated.

Therefore, a tax should be imposed on pass-through charities. Another simple example follows, illustrating the tax treatment of pass-through charities. For a pass-through charity, from every unit it collects, it remits a percentage immediately to the government. This percentage is based on the prior year's financial reports.

The income tax should be determined from expenses not used for charitable purposes. This includes marketing and certain salaries. The pass-through charity often contracts with a marketing firm or uses its employees to make phone calls, print advertisements, or run television and internet ads. These expenses, although often exorbitant, are ostensibly necessary to raise awareness and money. Salaries for successful pass-through charity directors and many employees are also very generous.

For income tax purposes, salaries would be divided into tiers like regular corporations. The salary earned by the top ten percent to the total salary is calculated. However, for non-profit corporations, an additional ratio is calculated – the salary of employees making more than some metric, like the mean salary for the nation, or a multiple of some national base salary, to the total salary. The maximum of the two ratios is used. The second test is necessary in cases where all employees are paid well above the norm. In a standard calculation, the top ten percent ratio would be deceptively low.

Table 23: Taxation of Pass-Through Charity		
Collections	1,000,000	
Income Tax	600,000	Tax rate 60%
Collections After Tax (line 1 minus 2)	400,000	
Marketing	140,000	
Salary of Top Ten/Above Average	100,000	
Salary of Remainder/Other Expenses	50,000	
Money Passed to Worthy Cause Activities	110,000	
Collections Less Expenses (line 3 minus lines 4,5,6 and 7)	0	If greater than 0, add to tax
Marketing plus Top Ten/Above Average Salaries	240,000	
Next Year's Tax Rate	60%	240,000/400,000

In this example, the current year's tax rate is equal to the prior year's tax rate. The pass-through is operating on a consistent basis.

Charitable expenses should not be a deductible item when determining income taxes. If they are, then contributions to a pass-through charity should be deductible only to the extent that the money is actually used for charitable purposes. In our simple example, the individual may only deduct 16 units for every 100 units donated (the sum of Money Passed to Worthy Cause Activities plus Salary of Remainder/Other Expenses, divided by Collections). An amount may be passed to a worthy cause that also spends money on marketing and exorbitant salaries. If this is the case, then the 16 units are further reduced.

SOLUTION: VALUE-ADDED TAX

A value-added tax, or VAT, is used in many countries instead of an income tax or as a supplement to the income tax. The VAT is imposed on every transaction.

For example, a baker wishes to sell apple pies. He must purchase apples, flour, yeast, eggs, and sugar. When he creates a pie, he has "added value" to the ingredients by applying his labor. When he then sells the pie, in addition to covering his expenses and his profit, he must charge the consumer a VAT.

Now, if the baker buys dough from another vendor instead of flour, yeast, and eggs, he must pay a VAT on the dough. To cover his VAT payment, he can choose to accept either lower profits or raise his prices to consumers.

If the baker sells his pies to a grocery store on a wholesale basis, the grocer pays the VAT on the same basis as consumers. Consumers buying pies from the grocer pay an additional VAT on the retail price because the grocer has presumably added value as well.

So, every step of every process carries a VAT.

In theory, one could use the VAT like the corporate income tax to incent corporations to pay higher middle-class salaries. Companies with a Company Management Share higher than the Standard Management Share would have to charge a higher VAT to their customers

Examine the two companies used as examples from the corporate income tax section of this manifesto:

Table 24: Calculation of VAT Rate using Dynamic Tax Principles		
	Company #1	Company #2
Standard Management Share	25%	25%
Company Management Share	10%	55%
Management Share Adjustment	(15%)	30%
Standard VAT Rate	15%	15%
Corporate VAT Rate	0%	45%

The Standard VAT Rate may vary by product. It is the government-determined VAT rate for a company adhering to distributing salary to its employees in line with the calculation of the Standard Management Share. These are the desired industry or company size standards. The formula for the Corporate VAT Rate may vary. In our simple example, we used Corporate VAT Rate = Standard VAT Rate plus Management Share Adjustment.

For every product Company #1 sells, the government takes no VAT. For every product Company #2 sells, the government imposes a 45% tax at the point of sale. If the two companies competed against one another, Company #1 would have a definite price advantage.

Using the VAT to encourage equitable corporate income distribution has certain drawbacks.

First is the horrible complexity. The VAT often varies by product. One would want to show the VAT to customers as a separately identified item on the bill so they would know which company is the better corporate steward. Audit and collection would be complex. However, in a future cashless society, the complexity can be managed. Every transaction would have a company code and product code, and the appropriate tax could be added.

Second, one would need to file salaries with the government to determine the Company Management Share. For a country relying solely on a VAT, this is a new reporting requirement. Once in place, implementing a corporate income tax system would be relatively easy.

Third, the VAT and company adjustments must be large enough to influence financial decisions. A VAT of 2% with an adjustment to 4% is probably not sufficiently large to influence buying decisions.

Fourth, the VAT is paid by customers. It is not a mechanism for taking money from a corporation. It merely takes business away based on price. Collecting negative VATs is not practical.

Fifth, a company with a dominant market position may not care how much VAT its customers must pay. A big company may be able to absorb some of the VAT and still be the market leader. If a large company's sales are not materially affected, then it can and will set salaries at any level it chooses.

Still, a VAT with a Management Share Adjustment is better than a VAT without one.

SOLUTION: SALES TAXES

Sales taxes are generally regressive taxes, imposed on retail sales, and paid by the ultimate consumer. To demonstrate its regressive character, let's use a simple example. Person #1 earns 500 units annually. Person #2 earns 5,000 units annually. Both must spend 400 units annually on self-maintenance. A sales tax of 3% is added to all expenditures. Each person saves the remainder.

Table 25: Simple Example of Effective Sales Tax Rate

	Person #1	Person #2
Earnings	500	5,000
Expenditures	400	400
Sales Tax	12	12
Remainder for Savings	88	4,588
Effective Tax Rate	2.40%	0.24%

The Effective Tax Rate is the Sales Tax divided by Earnings. In this example, Person #1 pays a much higher effective tax rate than Person #2. Person #1 would generally be considered middle-class. In reality, many items like food are not subject to the sales tax. Also, wealthy people spend their income on more than just bare necessities. But the regressive nature of the sales tax remains.

Sales taxes seem to be more palatable to the public than income taxes, but a society that wishes to promote the middle class will keep sales taxes to a minimum. The optimal solution is to abolish sales taxes since they are regressive and are not suitable to redistribute income or assets. If society insists on having a sales tax, then at a minimum food and medicine should be exempt. Taxing durable goods like appliances is regressive. The practice of taxing hotels and restaurants is probably acceptable since travel and vacation is a choice, and becoming more of a luxury. Finally, jurisdictions should consider taxing tuition. The tax might be imposed on tuitions above a certain threshold and would include a tax on donations and endowments. The tuition tax rate could be calculated along the lines of the Fair Distribution Tax, where institutions that pay their deans, regents, or other officers enormous amounts.

Tariffs are disguised sales taxes. They are taxes on the citizens of your country, levied on certain goods imported from other countries. Like a sales tax, the tariff is paid when a citizen purchases the affected good. The stated purpose of levying a tariff varies but usually involves unfair trade of some sort. Historically, tariffs have met little political opposition because they enhance government revenues.

SOLUTION: INDIVIDUAL TAXATION ON INVESTMENTS

Taxation on individuals has been established and implemented with the consent of the people. Through representative government and the legal system, taxation rules on both income and assets have been codified, published and legally enforced. Arguments to the contrary are specious.

In theory, most developed countries have a graduated progressive income tax. In theory, the tax rate on higher incomes and earnings should be greater than the tax rate on lower incomes and earnings. Wealthy taxpayers have more disposable income since the cost of basic self-maintenance as a percentage of total earnings is small. In practice, tax rates have not been progressive and tax rules have not been fair. Earnings from different sources have been taxed differently. Usually, income or earnings derived from sources primarily available to the wealthy have been given lower tax rates. The result has been a bell curve where the effective tax for the middle class is higher than the effective tax for either the rich or poor.

Some definitions are needed. The Marginal Tax Rate is the tax rate on a portion or tier of income. For example:

Individual #1 earns 8,000 units

Table 26: Example of Calculation of Effective Tax Rate using Income Tiers and Marginal Tax Rates

Income Tier	Marginal Tax Rate	Income within Tier	Tax
0 to 1,000	5%	1,000	50
1,000 to 3,000	15%	2,000	300
3,000 and above	25%	5,000	1,250
Total		8,000	1,600

The Effective Tax Rate is the total tax divided by total income. For Individual #1, the effective tax rate is 20% (1,600/8,000).

Individual #2 earns 16,000 units

Table 27: Example of Calculation of Effective Tax Rate using Income Tiers and Marginal Tax Rates			
Income Tier	Marginal Tax Rate	Income within Tier	Tax
0 to 1,000	5%	1,000	50
1,000 to 3,000	15%	2,000	300
3,000 and above	25%	13,000	3,250
Total		16,000	3,600

The effective tax rate for Individual #2 is 22.5% (3,600/16,000).

The marginal tax rates for the two individuals are the same. Individual #2 pays a higher effective tax rate since he earns more (has more earnings subject to the 25% marginal tax rate).

The notion of marginal tax rates could apply to individual taxes. The income tax system in the United States in 2020 has already evolved to the point where most (over 85%) individuals rely on software and tax preparers.

We can easily surmise that in the future, the government will know every individual's assets, and the categorization, valuation, and taxation will be computerized. The formulas, although potentially complex, should be transparent and completely objective. Public confidence in the taxation system is essential.

Different marginal tax rates should be applied to different sources of income. Society determines these tax rates and optimal rates will ultimately be determined partly by competition between countries or states for residents, production, and public services. Marginal tax rates may vary by type and size of income. For example, taxes on investments may be higher than taxes on income from working. Taxes on the value of government benefits should be considered, whether the benefits are direct payments, subsidies or services.

First, let's examine a fair method of taxing investment earnings. It follows the marginal tax concept. Let's start with an example of three individuals. They have 20,000, 200,000, and 2 million units of investments respectively covered by this part of the tax computation. They each earn a 5% return on their investment. We now determine the tax.

Table 28: Example of Graduated Method of Taxing Investment Earnings				
Investment Tier	Marginal Allowance	Person #1 20,000 units	Person #2 200,000 units	Person #3 2 million units
0 to 1,000	20%	200	200	200
1,000 to 10,000	15%	1,350	1,350	1,350
10,000 to 50,000	8%	800	3,200	3,200
50,000 to 250,000	3%		4,500	6,000
250,000 to 1,000,000	1%			7,500
1,000,000 to 5,000,000	0.25%			2,500
Over 5,000,000	0.1%			
Total Allowance		2,350	9,250	20,750
Actual Earnings at 5%		1,000	10,000	100,000
Taxable Earnings		0	750	79,250
Potential Carryforward		1,350	0	0
Tax Rate		80%	80%	80%
Tax		0	600	63,400

Taxable Earnings is Actual Earnings less the Total Allowance. The Carryforward is the unused Total Allowance. Depending on the investment, the government may or may not allow unused allowances to be carried into subsequent tax years.

This approach encourages fair reporting and valuation of assets. The higher the value of the asset, the higher the allowance. There is no depreciation (like for an office building or apartment complex) unless depreciation is warranted. Depreciation could be treated as an offset to investment income for tax purposes. Underreporting the value of an asset decreases the allowance available and increases the tax burden.

This approach rewards savings. The allowances on the first tier should be large enough to support assets in the second tier. In our example, the 200 unit allowance can support assets of up to 4,000 units (4,000 X 5% return = 200 units).

The government can set allowances at a level sufficient to support retirement savings. Individuals will save money if their savings are tax-free. Governments have long subscribed to a theory of taxing behavior they wish to discourage while offering tax incentives to behavior they wish to encourage. If the government wishes to encourage individual responsibility regarding savings, it needs to incent individual saving.

The government can set the tiers according to inflation. Tiers should be indexed, either set automatically or determined by regulation.

There may be classes of assets that receive no allowance, like investments in a hostile country or investments in products detrimental to health.

Neither long-term nor short-term assets receive preferential tax treatment. Because inflation (if any) is "baked" into the tiers and the annual valuation of assets, most taxes are based on current information.

Some types of investments are typically long-term. The most common is the primary residence. On average, homes are held for seven years, but some may be held for thirty years or more. Taxing an asset that has not been sold is inappropriate because no cash is available to pay the tax. So, it is inappropriate to tax a home annually based on the increase in the value of the property.

When a home is sold, there are typically several years of appreciation in the value since the time of the original purchase. This can be addressed by a system of carryforwards for this particular asset.

Again, a simple example illustrates the mechanism.

Table 29: Example of Income Tax and Allowances on Long Term Investments								
Time	Year 0	Year 1	Year 2	Year 3	Year 4	Year 5	Year 6	Year 7
Tier 1	0 to 250,000	0 to 262,500	0 to 275,625	0 to 289,406	0 to 303,877	0 to 319,070	0 to 335,024	0 to 351,775
Tier 2	250,000 to 1,000,000	262,500 to 1,050,000	275,625 to 1,102,500	289,406 to 1,157,625	303,877 to 1,215,506	319,070 to 1,276,282	335,024 to 1,340,096	351,775 to 1,407,100
Home Value	400,000	420,000	441,000	463,050	486,203	510,513	536,038	562,840
Tier 1 Allowance (5%)	12,500	13,125	13,782	14,470	15,194	15,954	16,751	
Tier 2 Allowance (3%)	4,500	4,725	4,961	5,210	5,470	5,743	6,031	
Total Allowance	17,500	17,850	18743	19,680	20,664	21,697	22,782	
Carryforward	17,500	34,850	53,593	73,272	93,936	115,633	138,414	

If the home is bought at the beginning of Year 0 for 400,000 units and sold at the beginning of Year 7 for 562,840 units, the gain is the difference (162,840 units). The Carryforward is 138,414 units, leaving a taxable amount of 24,426 units. If the tax rate on this type of investment were 20%, the tax would be 4,885 units.

There are a few important points regarding this valuation/tax methodology.

First, the government determines a fair increase in property values every year. In our simple example, this was 5% every year. This percentage determines the upper and lower bounds of each tier in each year. For example, the Year 2 Tier 2 bounds are 250,000 units X 1.05 X 1.05 = 275,625, and 1,000,000 X 1.05 X 1.05 = 1,102,500.

Second, the percentages used to determine successive upper and lower bounds should match the Tier 1 Allowance. (The government could set the allowance higher than the annual property increase, but should never set the Tier 1 Allowance lower.)

Third, the higher Tier Allowances could be set at a lower rate than the fair increase in property values. The difference between the Tier 1 Allowance and other Tier Allowances is essentially a source of income for a progressive tax system.

Fourth, this tax system specifically recognizes inflation and does not impose an inflation tax. If the Tier 2 Allowance in the example were set to 5%, the Carryforward at the end of Year 6 would have been 162,840 units and the taxable amount would have been 0 units. This is because the actual property gain was identical to the national average set by the government.

Fifth, if the property sold at a premium (above the national gain benchmark), the amount of the premium would be taxable. For example, if the property were sold for 600,000 units, the taxable amount in our example would have been (600,000 minus 400,000 = 200,000, less an allowance of 138,414 = 61,586 units). 37,160 is the gain from selling at a premium and 24,426 is the gain from imposing a progressive taxation system.

Sixth, this kind of tax system uses uniform rates by type of asset class. There is no arbitrary long term/short term differential. Taxes are imposed when a property is sold, so income is available to pay an income tax. Taxes are not imposed on inheritances. The carryforward on each asset could either be preserved, adjusted to zero, or set somewhere in between to determine the ultimate taxable value when the property is ultimately sold by an heir.

SOLUTION: PROPERTY AND CASUALTY INSURANCE PROVIDED ON A PARTICIPATING BASIS

Once upon a time, there was a fairly wealthy man whose father was a member of the House of Representatives for his state. The family was very well-connected politically. Beginning in the 1950s, he bought stock in automobile insurance companies and eventually gained a controlling interest in a few. In the 1960s and 1970s, automobile insurance was a product that a member of the middle class could purchase to cover liability or property costs or else forego insurance and accept the risks intrinsic to operating a motor vehicle on public roads. Many drivers chose to forego automobile insurance, especially if their cars were old or they had few assets to protect should they become a defendant in litigation. Many had other insurance, including health or disability coverage, to protect them in case of injury.

Shortly after acquiring the insurance company, the wealthy man and other owners of automobile insurance companies began lobbying the states (which had jurisdiction over insurance at the time) to pass legislation requiring the purchase of automobile insurance on every car. Proof of insurance would be required at annual renewal/tax time. The propaganda used to sell the public on the idea was that uninsured motorists were a cost to society because severe accidents would leave people unable to work. They would become wards of the state, requiring personal maintenance and health care. This might have been true, but it was a tiny cost relative to the "solution."

State legislatures are comprised of people – people with political connections. They, their friends and their relatives have consulting companies, legal firms, and insurance sales offices. Legislators have election funds and charities to which impacted businesses may contribute.

The type of automobile insurance passed in virtually every state was the most expensive to adjudicate and administer and was an absolute boon to insurance carriers. Legally, in every state except one, the middle-class consumer must buy liability insurance if he wishes to operate a vehicle. In case he hurts someone including himself, the insurance company will cover it. The consumer also must buy insurance that covers property damage. If he damages property including his own, the insurance policy must pay the claim. The insurance company pays the insured or a third party if the loss is the fault of its policyholder.

When an accident occurs, the insurance companies covering both parties become involved. As a matter of course, one or both deny responsibility, claiming it was the other driver's fault. If damage or liability has occurred, then the negotiating process between the insurer and the affected party begins. This process generally involves intensive labor over several weeks, which is very expensive.

There is a more economical way called "no-fault." In this case, the insurance company covers its policyholder for the expenses he or she has chosen to insure, no matter who was at fault. It eliminates lawyers, negotiators, and tort-based litigation.

The easiest way to trim rates is through regulatory enforcement of the loss ratio, which is simply the ratio of the claims paid to the premiums collected. It should come as no surprise that mandated coverages have the lowest loss ratios. For mandated liability coverage, the loss ratio is usually between 30% and 50%. This means that the insurance company keeps about 60 cents of every dollar it collects. Coverages that are not mandated, like collision, have a loss ratio between 70% and 80%, which are much more consumer-friendly.

Insurance companies routinely double cover but only pay claims on one policy. For example, a car hits a fence. The fence is insured under both automobile and homeowner policies, and premiums are collected for the risk on both. But should a policyholder file a claim, only the value of one fence (depreciated) is reimbursed to the insured.

Finally, automobile insurance is priced per automobile. If a family with two drivers has three cars, they pay three times. The real risk is the minimum of the number of drivers or the number of cars. Again, a middle-class driver who might need a spare car must pay an unfair amount on mandatory insurance.

What happened to the politically connected man who bought the insurance company? He managed to create an environment where almost every adult had to buy his product (maybe not necessarily from his company) every year, at prices at least twice the cost of the payouts, for an administratively burdensome plan. He also managed to select the safest drivers to insure. States created pools and substandard carriers to cover drivers with bad driving records. He became one of the richest men in the world.

What happened to the consumers? They were supposed to save money by not having to provide for those who became wards of the state. Well, it turns out that not everyone obeys the law and retains their automobile insurance. People still drive without insurance, and these people are more likely to get into an accident. They have been priced out of the market because they are bad drivers. They become wards of the state. Also, the mandated automobile insurance has rather low maximum lifetime benefits. Benefits for disability reach the maximum after two to five years. At that point, the insured drivers become wards of the state.

The middle class has saved nothing but has substantially less disposable income through mandated automobile insurance.

A better system is a voluntary, no-fault system. The middle-class consumer decides, based on his or her utility function, whether the cost of the insurance is worth the protection. Since insurance carriers would be forced to compete with a decision not to buy their product, their premiums would plummet. Claims would be processed in a highly efficient manner. Through word of mouth and the Internet, companies would be sensitive to their reputation. Middle-class disposable income would be maximized.

Also, all property and casualty insurance should be "participating." This means that the policyholders share with the insurance company in the financial performance of their line of business. The insurer is required to pay a dividend or rebate to the policyholders if it makes a profit.

In the United States of America, major medical health insurance was forced in 2010 to become participating by the federal government. The statutory minimum loss ratios range from 80% to 85%, depending on the size of the group purchasing the insurance. Measurements are made every calendar year. If the block of business experiences a 78% loss ratio, the company must return 2% of the premium to the insureds. If the block experiences a 90% loss ratio, the company takes a financial hit. There is no carry forward of losses. This law is not well-conceived and has already led to limited choices and unaffordable rates. To avoid ruin, companies must price the coverage at a 75% loss ratio, anticipating annual dividends.

The precedent exists that if the government requires citizens to purchase an item (health insurance), then that item must cost the citizen as little as possible. It is now time to apply that same principle to other insurance. The government requires automobile insurance for every driver, so the product must be as affordable as possible. Banks require homeowners' insurance to secure a mortgage, so that product must be affordable as well.

One purpose of this manifesto is to propose regulatory blueprints that all parties find acceptable. The following paragraphs contain a blueprint for offering property and casualty coverage that assures fair pricing and financial solvency.

A simple example illustrates the financial operation of property and casualty insurance. The company issues automobile or homeowners' coverage. The expected value of the risk is 100 units. The company charges 160 units to cover administrative costs, adverse deviation, and a super-sufficient margin whose purpose is to assure the company that it will not lose money. By regulation, the company must maintain a loss ratio (claims divided by premium) of 92% and must return any excess to the policyholders. Furthermore, the company must return 96% of investment earnings to the customers since the company is charging excessive rates and holding the funds due to be rebated or distributed to policyholders.

Table 30: Examples of Dividend Calculations for Participating Property and Casualty Insurance			
	Good Year	Bad Year	Terrible Year
Expected Losses	100	100	100
Standard Deviation	20	20	20
Administrative Expenses	5	5	5
Excess Margin	35	35	35
Total Premium	160	160	160
Actual Losses	69	124.2	151.8
Allowable Loss Ratio	92%	92%	92%
Company's Portion of Premium	75	135	165
Insurance Dividend	85	25	(5)
Investment Income	1	1	1
Allowable Company Share of Invest. Inc.	4%	4%	4%
Investment Dividend	0.96	0.96	0.96
Total Dividend	85.96	25.96	0.00
Loss Carryforward	0	0	4.04

The Total Premium is the sum of Expected Losses, one Standard Deviation, Administrative Expenses, and an Excess Margin to provide for financial stability.

Three scenarios are shown: a good year, a bad year, and a terrible year. The good year's actual performance was more than one standard deviation better than expected. The bad year's performance was more than one standard deviation worse than the expected performance. The terrible year is representative of a catastrophe, like a hurricane.

The Allowable Loss Ratio is set by regulation.

The Company's Portion of the Premium is the Actual Losses divided by the Allowable Loss Ratio. The higher the Actual Losses, the higher the Total Premium. This is equitable since administrative costs are concomitantly higher.

The Insurance Dividend is the Total Premium less the Company's Portion of the Premium.

The actual Investment Income in this example is 1 unit.

The Allowable Company Share of Investment Income is set by regulation. The vast majority of investment income should be returned to the policyholders.

The Investment Dividend is the Investment Income times one minus the Allowable Company Share of Investment Income. If investment income were negative, then the Investment Dividend would be zero. The company has a fiduciary responsibility to invest prudently, and any investment losses are solely company losses.

The Total Dividend is the sum of the Insurance Dividend and the Investment Dividend. In the case of a terrible year, the Total Dividend is zero, and any shortfalls are carried into subsequent years and will decrement future dividends.

SOLUTION: REGULATION OF INTEREST RATES CHARGED BY BANKS TO MIDDLE-CLASS CONSUMERS

In 2020, banks and other financial institutions in both the developed world and underdeveloped world receive deposits and make a variety of loans. Credit cards account for a significant portion of a bank's loan activity.

Historically, in the United States of America, each state had usury laws setting limits on the interest rates banks could charge. In the 1970s, as a result of high oil prices and ensuing inflation, interest rates on all types of loans and deposits soared. The prevailing interest rates started bumping up against the usury limits. States promptly repealed or vastly diminished their usury laws. This accommodation by the states was done in part because banks needed revenue to offset long-term real estate loans made at low locked-in rates. It also allowed banks to issue credit cards to less creditworthy customers, expanding their customer base. The higher interest rates were intended to offset higher defaults.

Also, until the 1970s, the spread between the rates that banks paid on deposits and the rates banks charged on loans was rather modest – generally 2%.

In the 1990s, interest rates began to dramatically decrease. However, the usury laws were never reinstated. Banks continued charging 18% to 24% on credit cards even though the low-rate real estate loans had been paid. Credit rating bureaus began business, supplying banks with a scoring and reporting system on individual customers. Banks gained access to information on consumer debt repayment.

By 2020, the interest rates banks paid on deposits were less than 2% and the average spread between loans and deposits swelled to over 7%. Banks retained the lion's share of the return on the loans. Several legislative attempts were made to curb credit card rates but each failed. Instead of banks competing to provide consumers the most favorable deposit and loan rates, they paid out as little and charged as much as they possibly could.

Credit cards are unsecured loans. Home and automobile loans are secured loans, meaning if payments are not made, the bank can take the underlying asset. Unsecured loans carry a greater risk of default so the interest rate charged is legitimately higher than a secured loan.

In 2020 in developed countries, a mature credit rating industry exists. Several corporations collect consumer payment histories and traceable assets. Banks routinely use this information to determine eligibility and term for a loan. The more dependable the borrower, the easier it is for him or her to get a loan, and the lower the interest rate than a less creditworthy borrower.

Longer loans require higher interest rates because the distant future is more uncertain than the near future. Interest rates may change, inflation may rise, a recession may occur, or a particular customer may face a loss of employment or financial difficulty and default. Banks often maintain that credit cards are open-ended loans, extending over the life of a customer, and therefore should logically carry the highest rates.

One must understand the concept of duration, the measure of the length of a loan based on the expected cash flows and a desired rate of return. It is used in bonds, which are loans from consumers to corporations or government entities, to assist in financial planning. Credit cards have a relatively short duration.

A simple duration calculation is shown below.

The first example is a loan of 10,000 units (which could be a credit card) at 5%. The loan is repaid with level annual payments of 802.43.

Table 31: Calculation of the Duration of a Loan Repaid over 20 Years – Level Payments at 5%				
(A) Year	(B) Payment	(C) Outstanding Balance	(D) Yield	(E) (A)X(B)X(D)
0		10,000.00	1.000000	
1	802.43	9,697.57	0.970874	779.06
2	802.43	9,380.02	0.942596	1,512.73
3	802.43	9,046.59	0.915142	2,203.01
4	802.43	8,696.49	0.888487	2,851.79
5	802.43	8,328.88	0.862609	3,460.92
6	802.43	7,942.90	0.837484	4,032.14
7	802.43	7,537.61	0.813092	4,567.14
8	802.43	7,112.06	0.789409	5,067.57
9	802.43	6,665.24	0.766417	5,534.96
10	802.43	6,196.07	0.744094	5,970.83
11	802.43	5,703.44	0.722421	6,367.62
12	802.43	5,186.18	0.701380	6,753.70
13	802.43	4,643.06	0.680951	7,103.41
14	802.43	4,072.79	0.661118	7,427.01
15	802.43	3,474.00	0.641862	7,725.74
16	802.43	2,845.27	0.623167	8,000.77
17	802.43	2,185.10	0.605016	8,253.22
18	802.43	1,491.92	0.587395	8,484.18
19	802.43	764.09	0.570286	8,694.68
20	802.43	0.00	0.553676	8,885.72
Total	16,048.60			113,685.18
Duration	Total (E) / Total (B)	7.08		

The second example is a loan of 10,000 units made at 20%. The loan is repaid with level annual payments of 2,053.56.

Table 32: Calculation of the Duration of a Loan Repaid over 20 Years – Level Payments at 20%				
(A)	(B)	(C)	(D)	(E)
Year	Payment	Outstanding Balance	Yield	(A)X(B)X(D)
0		10,000.00	1.000000	
1	2,053.56	9,946.44	0.970874	1,993.75
2	2,053.56	9,882.17	0.942596	3,871.35
3	2,053.56	9,805.04	0.915142	5,637.89
4	2,053.56	9,712.49	0.888487	7,298.25
5	2,053.56	9,601.43	0.862609	8,857.09
6	2,053.56	9,468.15	0.837484	10,318.95
7	2,053.56	9,308.22	0.813092	11,688.13
8	2,053.56	9,116.31	0.789409	12,968.79
9	2,053.56	8,886.01	0.766417	14,164.94
10	2,053.56	8,609.65	0.744094	15,280.42
11	2,053.56	8,278.02	0.722421	16,318.89
12	2,053.56	7,880.07	0.701380	17,283.91
13	2,053.56	7,402.52	0.680951	18,178.87
14	2,053.56	6,829.47	0.661118	19,007.03
15	2,053.56	6,141.80	0.641862	19,771.53
16	2,053.56	5,316.80	0.623167	20,475.37
17	2,053.56	4,326.36	0.605016	21,121.44
18	2,053.56	3,138.07	0.587395	21,712.50
19	2,053.56	1,712.13	0.570286	22,251.21
20	2,053.56	0.00	0.553676	22,740.13
Total	41,071.20			290,940.44
Duration	Total (E) / Total (B)	7.08		

The third example is a loan of 10,000 units made at 20%. The loan is repaid with 500 units per year plus interest on the outstanding balance.

Table 33: Calculation of the Duration of a Loan Repaid over 20 Years – Level Principle Repayments plus Interest at 20%				
(A) Year	(B) Payment	(C) Outstanding Balance	(D) Yield	(E) (A)X(B)X(D)
0		10,000.00	1.000000	
1	2,500.00	9,500.00	0.970874	2,427.18
2	2,400.00	9,000.00	0.942596	4,524.46
3	2,300.00	8,500.00	0.915142	6,314.48
4	2,200.00	8,000.00	0.888487	7,818.69
5	2,100.00	7,500.00	0.862609	9,057.39
6	2,000.00	7,000.00	0.837484	10,049.81
7	1,900.00	6,500.00	0.813092	10,814.12
8	1,800.00	6,000.00	0.789409	11,367.49
9	1,700.00	5,500.00	0.766417	11,726.18
10	1,600.00	5,000.00	0.744094	11,905.50
11	1,500.00	4,500.00	0.722421	11,919.95
12	1,400.00	4,000.00	0.701380	11,783.18
13	1,300.00	3,500.00	0.680951	11,508.08
14	1,200.00	3,000.00	0.661118	11,106.78
15	1,100.00	2,500.00	0.641862	10,590.72
16	1,000.00	2,000.00	0.623167	9,970.67
17	900.00	1,500.00	0.605016	9,256.75
18	800.00	1,000.00	0.587395	8,458.48
19	700.00	500.00	0.570286	7,584.80
20	600.00	0.00	0.553676	6,644.11
Total	31,000.00			184,828.83
Duration	Total (E) / Total (B)	5.96		

The fourth example is a loan of 10,000 units made at 20%. The loan is repaid with interest only for 20 years, when the principal is repaid.

Table 34: Calculation of the Duration of a Loan Repaid over 20 Years – Interest Only at 20%, Principal Repaid after 20 Years

(A) Year	(B) Payment	(C) Outstanding Balance	(D) Yield	(E) (A)X(B)X(D)
0		10,000.00	1.000000	
1	2,000.00	10,000.00	0.970874	1,941.75
2	2,000.00	10,000.00	0.942596	3,770.38
3	2,000.00	10,000.00	0.915142	5,490.85
4	2,000.00	10,000.00	0.888487	7,107.90
5	2,000.00	10,000.00	0.862609	8,626.09
6	2,000.00	10,000.00	0.837484	10,049.81
7	2,000.00	10,000.00	0.813092	11,383.28
8	2,000.00	10,000.00	0.789409	12,630.55
9	2,000.00	10,000.00	0.766417	13,795.50
10	2,000.00	10,000.00	0.744094	14,881.88
11	2,000.00	10,000.00	0.722421	15,893.27
12	2,000.00	10,000.00	0.701380	16,833.12
13	2,000.00	10,000.00	0.680951	17,704.73
14	2,000.00	10,000.00	0.661118	18,511.30
15	2,000.00	10,000.00	0.641862	19,255.86
16	2,000.00	10,000.00	0.623167	19,941.34
17	2,000.00	10,000.00	0.605016	20,570.56
18	2,000.00	10,000.00	0.587395	21,146.21
19	2,000.00	10,000.00	0.570286	21,670.87
20	12,000.00	0.00	0.553676	132,882.18
Total	50,000.00			394,087.42
Duration	Total (E) / Total (B)	7.88		

It is possible to set a duration for every type of loan or investment, including credit cards. Credit card durations are actually quite low. Even a calculation assuming no principal payments for 20 years gives a duration less than 8 years.

To assist the middle class, governments need to set limits on credit card and other loan interest rates. These limits must apply to every financial institution. There must be no loopholes. Competition does not seem to be an effective mechanism to contain usurious interest rates. A logical, meaningful regulation of interest rates would be as follows.

A base rate would be set. This rate would be defined by lengthy legislative consensus, but would probably be the risk-free rate that government bonds would pay or the short term rate that banks charge on interbank loans.

The allowable interest rates would then depend on the base rate. The table below shows the increments to the base rate. The increments are illustrative. The actual increments would again be set according to legislative consensus.

Table 35: Example of Increments to the Statutory Base Rate for Secured Loans

			Creditworthiness		
Duration	Marginal	Poor	Average	Good	Exceptional
0-1.5 Years	1.5%	1.25%	1.0%	0.75%	0.5%
1.5-3.5 Years	2.5%	2.25%	2.0%	1.75%	1.5%
3.5-6.5 Years	3.25%	3.0%	2.5%	2.0%	1.75%
6.5-9.5 Years	4.0%	3.5%	3.0%	2.5%	2.0%
9.5-14.5 Years	4.75%	4.0%	3.5%	3.0%	2.25%
14.5 Years and Longer	6.5%	5.5%	4.5%	3.5%	2.5%

Table 36: Example of Increments to the Statutory Base Rate for Unsecured Loans

			Creditworthiness		
Duration	Marginal	Poor	Average	Good	Exceptional
0-1.5 Years	4.0%	3.75%	3.5%	3.25%	3.0%
1.5-3.5 Years	5.0%	4.75%	4.5%	4.25%	4.0%
3.5-6.5 Years	5.75%	5.5%	5.0%	4.5%	4.25%
6.5-9.5 Years	6.5%	6.0%	5.5%	5.0%	4.5%
9.5-14.5 Years	7.25%	6.5%	6.0%	5.5%	4.75%
14.5 Years and Longer	9.0%	8.0%	7.0%	6.0%	5.0%

Also in 2020, credit card companies charged merchants 1% to 3% of each purchase. Retailers simply increased prices to cover the fees, again to the detriment of the middle class. Any regulation limiting interest rates that financial institutions can charge needs to include these charges in the calculation of measured rates.

If a financial institution exceeded the maximum interest charge, the penalty should be a return to the consumer of three times the difference (actual interest charged less interest charged based on the statutory maximum) in addition to an excise tax of three times the difference. Another proposed reform is an excise tax on the amount charged to merchants of 150% of the amount charged.

We can hope that, as technology improves and is distributed throughout society, digital purchases will become the norm and the convenience of credit or debit cards will no longer warrant a fee. Merchants will have the technology to charge individual consumers according to their method of payment. Consumers then can choose the cheapest method.

THE MIDDLE CLASS AND INFLATION

Inflation is the increase in prices over time.

Inflation is both a cause and a symptom of economic changes. In 2020, governments in all developed countries embrace inflation as desirable and citizens have come to expect it. The unofficial target is 2% per year.

While moderate inflation benefits the government under certain circumstances, it harms the middle class in the short and long terms. This is another instance where incentives for government and the middle class move in opposite directions.

Inflation benefits a government that levies an income tax (under current tax law). In theory, banks pay an interest rate equal to the sum of the inflation rate and the real rate of return. A simple example follows. An individual deposits 1,000 units for one year with a bank. Because the inflation rate is 2%, and investors demand a 1% real rate of return, the bank pays a total interest of 3%. The income tax rate is 15%.

Table 37: Calculation of the Real Rate of Return under Inflation	
Bank deposit	1,000 units
Interest Paid – 3%	30 units
Inflation Rate – 2%	20 units
Real Rate of Return - 1%	10 units

At the end of the year, the individual has 1,030 units. He or she then must pay income tax on the 30 units. The tax is 4.5 units, leaving the individual with 1,025.5 units. Because of inflation, the 1,025.5 units are only worth 1,005.4 units at the end of the year (1,025.5/1.02). The actual real rate of return was only half of one percent.

Why the reduction in the actual real rate of return? Because the individual pays an income tax on inflation. In this example, the individual pays income tax of 4.5 units, of which 3.0 units are on inflation and 1.5 units are on the real rate of return. The portion of the individual's tax obligation due to inflation exceeds the tax obligation on the increase in the asset.

Furthermore, the real tax rate on interest actually approaches 50%. At the end of the year, the individual has increased his purchasing power by 5.4 units. He must pay 4.5 units in taxes, which is 45% of the real rate of return (4.5/10). He pays almost as much in taxes as he receives in purchasing power. This simple example represents the real world in many countries with a low income tax rate. If the income tax rate were 30%, then virtually all of the real return would be given to the government.

Inflation benefits a government that carries debt, which includes most governments worldwide. The real cost of the debt depends on the inflation rate used in the present value calculation. 1,000 units today are worth less than 1,000 units 5 years from now. Consider another simple example. A government needs to borrow money, so it issues a 1,000 unit bond paying 3% per year, maturing at face value in 5 years. It assumes inflation will be 2% per year.

Table 38: Calculation of the Real Rate of Return on a Government Bond

(1)	(2)	(3)	(4)	(5)	(6)	(7)	(8)
Year	Present Value at 2%	Payments at 3% per Year, No Tax	Payments Adjusted for Inflation	Payments at 3% per Year, 15% Tax	Payments Adjusted for Inflation	Payments at 3% per Year, 30% Tax	Payments Adjusted for Inflation
1	0.9804	30	29.41	25.5	25.00	21	20.59
2	0.9612	30	28.84	25.5	24.51	21	20.18
3	0.9423	30	28.27	25.5	24.03	21	19.79
4	0.9238	30	27.72	25.5	23.56	21	19.40
5	0.9057	1,030	932.90	1,025.5	928.82	1,021	924.75
Total			1,047.14		1,025.92		1,004.71
Annual Rate of Return			0.93%		0.51%		0.09%

In the table above, column 4 equals column 2 times column 3, column 6 equals column 2 times column 5, and column 8 equals column 2 times column 7.

Column 3 shows the government repayment schedule of the bond. Column 5 reduces the interest component of the repayment by 15%, and column 7 reduces the interest component by 30%, which are the income tax rates.

The table above shows that the real cost of government borrowing is far less than the stated nominal rate. Longer bond durations show a similar pattern.

The following table is identical to the previous table, except inflation ticks up to 4%, a rate higher than the bond coupon rate.

Table 39: Calculation of the Real Rate of Return on a Government Bond when Inflation Exceeds the Bond Interest Rate

(1) Year	(2) Present Value at 4%	(3) Payments at 3% per Year, No Tax	(4) Payments Adjusted for Inflation	(5) Payments at 3% per Year, 15% Tax	(6) Payments Adjusted for Inflation	(7) Payments at 3% per Year, 30% Tax	(8) Payments Adjusted for Inflation
1	0.9615	30	28.85	25.5	24.52	21	20.19
2	0.9246	30	27.74	25.5	23.58	21	19.42
3	0.8890	30	26.67	25.5	22.67	21	18.67
4	0.8548	30	25.64	25.5	21.80	21	17.95
5	0.8219	1,030	846.58	1,025.5	842.89	1,021	839.19
Total			955.48		935.45		915.42
Annual Rate of Return			(0.91%)		(1.33%)		(1.75%)

In the above scenario, the real cost of government borrowing is negative, meaning that it is advantageous for the government to borrow. It borrows from the middle class, the financially disadvantaged party in this transaction.

Inflation also harms the middle class through its destabilizing effect on business. In an inflationary environment, a business owner is pressured by higher prices for goods, a demand for higher wages from employees and higher prices for personal expenditures. A business owner may or may not be able to raise prices on the goods or services he produces to meet all three demands.

The following example with three different businesses illustrates this point. In Year 1, they have identical earnings. The businesses have no control over the cost of goods. Lines labeled Personal Expenditures and Personal Savings refer to the business owner's expenditures and savings. The business owner receives all of the Net Business Earnings and in this example has no control over Personal Expenditures.

Table 40: Examples of the Effects of Inflation on Business Financial Performance (Year 1)			
Year 1	Business A	Business B	Business C
Business Income	1,000	1,000	1,000
Cost of Goods	200	200	200
Cost of Labor	700	700	700
Net Business Earnings	100	100	100
Personal Expenditures	80	80	80
Personal Savings	20	20	20

In the table above, Net Business Earnings is calculated as Business Income less Cost of Goods less Cost of Labor. Personal Savings is calculated as Net Business Earnings less Personal Expenditures.

In Year 2, the three businesses are now in an economy with a 5% inflation rate. Business A can raise its prices with inflation. Business B was able to be proactive, raising its prices by 10% in anticipation of a 10% inflation that did not materialize. Business C was unable to raise its prices due to competitive pressures.

Year 2 earnings for each business are shown below.

Table 41: Examples of the Effects of Inflation on Business Financial Performance (Year 2)			
Year 2	Business A	Business B	Business C
Business Income	1,050	1,100	1,000
Cost of Goods	210	210	210
Cost of Labor	735	735	700
Net Business Earnings	105	155	90
Personal Expenditures	84	84	84
Personal Savings	21	71	6

Business A illustrates the case in which all values increase by the inflation rate. The status quo is maintained, with no winners or losers. The wages of middle-class workers, denoted by the line labeled Cost of Labor, increase with inflation. Thus, workers are neither adversely nor favorably affected by inflation. Any of the lines for Business B or C in Year 2 should be compared to the corresponding line for Business A Year 2, which is the new base case.

For Business B, labor costs increase by the inflation rate, and no more. The labor market only demands an increase in wages equal to the inflation rate. Any employee of Business B dissatisfied with working for a company where business income outpaces wage growth can be replaced by a new worker from the labor market. So the cost of labor in Year 2 for Business B is identical to the cost of labor in Year 2 for Business A.

Because it could raise its prices, Business B has 50 more units of Business Income than Business A. These 50 units flow to the business owner, who might purchase an asset or invest in additional business opportunities.

For Business C, labor costs do not increase from the prior year. The business owner was unable to raise his prices in Year 2, so he could not increase employee wages. Business C will probably lose workers and replace them with less-skilled members of the labor market who will accept lower salaries. Alternatively, Business C may reduce the number of employees. The cost of labor in Year 2 for Business C is identical to the cost of labor in Year 1 for Business C.

Because it could not raise prices, Business C has 50 fewer units of Business Income than Business A. Employees (Labor) must absorb 35 units of the shortfall and the owner must reduce his savings by 15 units. The employees experience a pay freeze while the owner sees an actual pay cut.

This simple example illustrates some important points.

First, inflation destabilizes business, labor, and the economy in general.

Second, in an inflationary economy, the business owners tend to be winners and the middle class tends to be losers. Inflation helps concentrate assets in the hands of the few.

Third, some may argue that Business B could and would give workers a 10% pay increase. The earnings would be represented in the table below. Overall labor and the economy are unaffected by inflation.

Table 42: Example of the Effects of Inflation on Business B (Year 2) if the Business Chose to Increase its Cost of Labor	
Year 2	Business B
Business Income	1,100
Cost of Goods	210
Cost of Labor	770
Net Business Earnings	120
Personal Expenditures	84
Personal Savings	36

This argument is flawed because the economy is not a zero-sum game. Winners and losers do not balance each other out because the size of the economy changes every year. The number of people in year two usually exceeds the number of people in year one. The distribution of businesses and the skill level of labor also changes. The size of each business and the market share each business controls also contribute to the picture. There may be one big winner and a hundred little losers.

Then there are also funds labeled Personal Savings. These funds could be invested in a foreign market, or similar funds arising in a foreign economy could be invested domestically. The economy is not a closed system. As seen from the example, the business owner has the greatest variability in income (except when an employee loses his job). Human nature and the operation of the utility function suggests that the distribution of funds in Business B - Year 2 would most resemble the case where the Cost of Labor is 735 units.

If inflation is bad, then is deflation good?

The financial effects of deflation on consumer savings, interest, and income taxes will be explored using analogous simple examples.

Deflation does not benefit a government that levies an income tax (under current tax law). The consumer's purchasing power increases tax-free. In deflationary times, banks still must pay interest or the consumer will simply keep his or her cash.

The simple example is modified. An individual deposits 1,000 units for one year. Now the deflation rate is 2%, and investors demand a 0.5% nominal rate of return on their money, which the bank pays. The income tax rate is 15%.

Table 43: Calculation of the Real Rate of Return under Deflation	
Bank deposit	1,000 units
Interest Paid – 0.5%	5 units
Inflation Rate – (2%)	(20) units
Real Rate of Return – 2.5%	25 units

At the end of the year, the individual has 1,005 units. He then must pay income tax on the 5 units. The tax is 0.75 units, leaving the individual with 1,004.25 units. Because of deflation, the 1,004.25 units are worth 1,024.75 units at the end of the year (1,004.25/0.98). The actual real rate of return was 2.475%. This benefits the middle-class investor much more than an inflationary economy.

Results are similar when a government carries debt. The real cost of the debt to the government is higher under deflation and the real return to investors holding government debt is also higher.

The relationship between business and labor under deflation is very different from the relationship under inflation. The economic environments causing or perpetuating inflation or deflation are very different. Under deflation, productivity becomes more important. Middle-class labor will strive to maintain their nominal earnings from the prior year. They will increase their hours worked or improve their skill levels.

The following table illustrates the impact of deflation on labor and the business owner when productivity is allowed to increase.

Table 44: Examples of the Effects of Deflation and Productivity on Business Financial Performance (Years 1 and 2)

	Year 1	Year 2, same productivity	Year 2, increased productivity
Business Income	1,000	950	1,000
Cost of Goods	200	190	200
Cost of Labor	700	665	700
Net Business Earnings	100	95	100
Personal Expenditures	80	76	76
Personal Savings	20	19	24

Column 3 represents the scenario where prices and wages decrease 5% from the prior year. This can be thought of as a new base, where everyone's standard of living is maintained.

Column 4 represents the alternative where the productivity of labor increases to maintain its wages. Business Income is also maintained, not because the price per item sold increases, but because the number of items produced and sold increases. Since the business produces more items, it needs more raw materials, so its Cost of Goods rises with the increase in the amount of raw materials purchased.

The previous example helps illustrate the following two important points:

First, in a deflationary period where productivity rises, the middle-class standard of living also improves. In our example, the status quo situation produced middle-class wages of 665 units in Year 2. The middle class was better off by 35 units.

Second, in this environment, the business owner's standard of living also improves, usually by a wider margin. In our example, the middle-class standard of living improved by 5.3% (700/665-1) while the business owner's personal savings improved by 26% (24/19-1).

A related issue is the masking of productivity gains in the inflation rate. Refer to the simple example from the inflationary environment.

Year 2 earnings for each business, assuming no productivity increases, are repeated:

Table 45: Examples of the Effects of Inflation on Business Financial Performance (Year 2)			
Year 2	Business A	Business B	Business C
Business Income	1,050	1,100	1,000
Cost of Goods	210	210	210
Cost of Labor	735	735	700
Net Business Earnings	105	155	90
Personal Expenditures	84	84	84
Personal Savings	21	71	6

Now assume a 2% productivity increase. Labor is sensitive to inflation and will try to bring its wages up to maintain its standard of living.

Year 2 earnings for each business, assuming a 2% productivity increase, are shown:

Table 46: Examples of the Effects of Inflation and Productivity on Business Financial Performance (Year 2)

Year 2	Business A	Business B	Business C
Business Income	1,071	1,122	1,020
Cost of Goods	214	214	214
Cost of Labor	735	735	714
Net Business Earnings	122	173	92
Personal Expenditures	84	84	84
Personal Savings	38	89	8

Since labor is "complacent," the business owners can siphon off the financial benefits of productivity increases. Only Business C is forced to share the productivity increase since its Cost of Labor is below market.

Some "experts" hold the opinion that deflation is undesirable because it will cause consumers to defer purchasing items in hopes of ultimately paying a lower price. The decisions to defer purchases lead to an economic slowdown. This is of course nonsense.

We have historical examples of deflation and can look at its effects on the middle class.

First, look at cellular phones, computers, and other electronics. Middle-class consumers do not wait for a price decrease to purchase a new cellphone. They know technology improves every year because it has for at least the past 20 years. When a new cellphone model comes out, they know its price in one year will be less than the current price. Do consumers wait a year before buying the new model? No. They rush to purchase the latest model. Often consumers must add their names to a waiting list to acquire the newest, most expensive model, bypassing older, cheaper models sitting on the shelves unsold.

Deflation in electronics has been an absolute boon to the middle class. A huge variety of products are available through various digital platforms, including word processing, spreadsheets, presentations, design, engineering, medical technology, and law enforcement. Productivity has increased by orders of magnitude. The energy efficiency of electronic devices has also increased dramatically.

Second, from 1820 to 1900, most of the world experienced deflation due to the Industrial Revolution. In the late 1700s and early 1800s, machines were developed to make fabric. These machines first ran on water power, then steam power. The technology of metal fabrication was perfected in terms of strength, precision, and standardization. Other technological innovations transformed many industries, aided by a patent system that protected intellectual property.

Deflation became manifest in agriculture and mining. New technology increased yields, forcing farmers and miners to produce more and more to maintain their standard of living. Many were less than thrilled with the situation.

Trade, transportation, and business surged. Items like clothing or cooking utensils became very affordable because they were mass-produced. The middle class flourished during these years. Average income increased while prices decreased.

From 1870 through 1890, the world economy flourished at an unbelievable pace. Deflation ran 3% per year. Real GDP growth was an astounding 7% per year. Everyone became richer – the rich, the poor and the middle class. Major technological developments during this time included steel casting, electric power grids, light bulbs, electric engines, rubber, and chemicals. The number of family farms in the United States grew from about 1 million in 1800 to 6 million in 1900.

The Communist Manifesto was written in 1848. Subsequent economic developments and evidence seem to have been ignored by steadfast adherents to the ideology.

Third, from 1900 to 1975, oil was a determinant of economic growth. Transportation became dependent on gasoline. The oil companies consolidated into a few large corporations with considerable market leverage. The large oil companies set the price they paid for a barrel of crude oil. They also set the price of a gallon or liter of gasoline at the pump.

From 1900 until World War I, the price of oil fluctuated modestly around 75¢ a barrel. During WWI, the price shot up to $3.00 a barrel. The price declined steadily until the Great Depression in 1933. It stayed between $1.00 and $1.10 a barrel until the end of World War II. From 1947 until 1970, the price of a barrel of oil was fixed at $1.80 to $1.90 a barrel. There was a 20-year span when the price of energy, an important part of the economy, remained unchanged.

The post-World War II period saw steady GDP growth and a further improvement in middle-class economic conditions. Prices stabilized and a spirit of optimism prevailed.

Turning to the future, addressing inflation and its adverse impact on the middle class, society should demand, and governments should take the following steps:

First, change income tax laws so no one pays a tax on inflation. One mechanism was addressed earlier in this manifesto. Another would be to exempt from taxation the first x% of investment earnings, where "x" is twice the prior year's inflation rate. If a taxpayer earned less than x%, the government should provide a rebate of the difference between x% times total invested assets and actual investment earnings. This would protect the middle class from inflation caused by and fostered by the government.

Second, change monetary policy so that the target inflation rate is 0%.

Third, reduce the national debt to zero. If the government is not a borrower, it has no incentive to devalue future currency. If the government is not a borrower, it does not compete with the private sector for funds. Without government as a steady customer, the institutions currently lending money to governments might act more favorably toward consumers. Governments might act less favorably toward financial institutions.

For the future, we should remember that inflation or deflation is both a cause and a symptom. Deflation comes from an increase in productivity. We have seen from the past that when mankind applied automation and technology, the price of clothing fell, the price of steel fell, the price of electronics fell, and middle-class wages increased. Deflation is usually not a symptom of an economic slowdown. It usually indicates a financial adjustment due to improved technology and productivity.

Productivity increases are still possible. In the future, we will talk to our computers instead of typing on a keyboard. Customer service will rely even more on artificial intelligence. Telemedicine will mean a few clicks to address a health issue.

The intelligence that goes into technology should be harnessed by governments to create good policy, not just to provide good service.

THE MIDDLE CLASS AND THE NATURE AND SIZE OF GOVERNMENT

Decision theory and actual conditions show that consensus evaluation and judgment are superior to autocratic decision-making. This phenomenon is shown in simple situations when people are asked to estimate marbles in a jar. The group average is very close to the actual number. Everyone in the group brings their own unique experiences, background, perceptions, and analytical abilities. Some people have a "feel" for the best course of action while others rely on hard data, evidence, or market research.

Good ideas and products are rapidly adopted and propagated. In Karl Marx's time, shoes were interchangeable, meaning there was no left or right shoe. Once someone conceived and developed complementary shoes, the fit was so superior that it became the norm. The idea and product rapidly spread to the thousands of shoemakers. Every shoemaker had access to the same market information and each produced a slightly different product.

Today, corporations behave in the same manner. Within an industry, every corporation has access to the same market information – what people want. Individual corporate strengths and weaknesses, abilities, and limitations also play a part in decision making. Management usually makes the decisions and not everyone comes to the same conclusion. The more corporations or participants there are in an industry, the more diverse the product offerings, and the higher the probability that the optimal solutions will be achieved. It is pure probability. The consensus process is at the corporate level, between competing corporations. Over time, corporations replicate successful ideas while discarding unsuccessful products.

This environment is healthiest for the middle class. There are opportunities for innovation, opportunities for manufacturing, and opportunities for technological improvement. These exist even within the confines of a corporation. Also, most innovations come from smaller entities and rarely from large corporations. Large corporations eventually copy, purchase, or license the rights to new and successful ideas.

Governments tend to be monopolistic. Consequently, innovation is slow. Remember that a government is not a physical entity but rather a collection of people. People in government tend to enjoy exercising control over others. Many government workers will divulge that their managers actively desire to expand their departments, increase their importance, and as a result increase their pay grades. They are supposed to be civil servants but do not see themselves as such.

Left unchecked, government departments and regional offices can expand staffing without really adding to the workload. This causes a lot of idle time. An old joke from the 1930s tells that a man once visited the U. S. Department of Agriculture and saw a bureaucrat sitting at his desk, crying. When the visitor asked what the matter was, the bureaucrat sobbed: "My farmer died."

Many government employees are attracted to the stability of a government position with duties that may not require much effort to perform. Pay raises are guaranteed and pay grades often depend on years of service. While nothing is inherently wrong with this job paradigm, unused labor is not optimal for society.

Government positions are usually middle-class jobs. In many countries, government jobs are at the upper end of the middle class, sought after not only for pay and stability but also for the opportunity to commit graft. Leaving money at a bureaucrat's desk or surreptitiously handing him or her an envelope containing money in exchange for a routine document is not unusual and often expected.

Throughout the world, the cost of doing business requires political contributions to elected officials and families of high-ranking bureaucrats. This supplants funds that could be used for middle-class employment. Many jurisdictions address graft, often in incongruous ways. For example, an anti-corruption statute in the state of Maine declares that the act of offering a bribe to a government official is a felony, but if the official accepts the bribe, he or she is only guilty of a misdemeanor.

Intuitively, the size and nature of government influence the economy. The United States of America can offer unique evidence of this. Many towns in the United States lie on the border of two states. Texarkana, Texas and Texarkana, Arkansas are familiar examples. The two towns have the same population composition and geographic location. The only differences are state taxation and services. It is obvious to a tourist which side of the border he or she is on. The town in the state with lower taxes has a bustling economy while its counterpart across the border is economically depressed. Even a small tax differential seems to matter. Jobs and the middle class migrate to the state with lower taxes.

It should stand to reason that lower taxes foster a vibrant middle class. There are of course certain necessary government functions that must be maintained.

To gauge the financial impact of government on the rest of the economy, examine the Gross Domestic Product (GDP) by category. A government does not produce income. It redistributes income. It provides necessary services, like law enforcement or infrastructure maintenance. Many of the other services it performs should be periodically examined to determine if they are still needed and if they can be delivered more efficiently.

For example, if government as a percentage of GDP is 15%, then the remaining 85% of the economy must fund it, resulting in a necessary support rate of 17.65% (15%/85%). If the government's share of GDP rose to 20%, either by expanding government or shrinking the rest of the economy, the necessary support rate would be 25% (20%/80%).

The support rate may be thought of as an overall tax rate. The non-government part of the economy is taxed to support the government part of the economy. The support rate may also be thought of in terms of the cost of goods and services (price). To pay the tax, the non-government part of the economy must increase prices by the amount of the support rate.

With a government share of GDP at 20%, the price of every item would include a markup of 25%. Government expansion from 15% to 20% of GDP would increase prices by 7.35%. The increase in price crowds out income for other uses and diminishes the middle-class standard of living. Mathematically, one sees that higher taxes are detrimental to the middle class. The converse, that lower taxes are beneficial to the middle class, is also true.

Growth in government leads to higher taxes. Companies must raise their prices to consumers by the amount of the direct tax increase and by the amount that their cost of goods has risen because their suppliers are obligated to do the same. The consumer pays for bigger government primarily through higher prices and secondarily through higher personal taxes. The consumer might not even realize the magnitude of the cost of larger government because the consumer only examines his or her tax return.

The cost of compliance with government regulations can be material to downright onerous. Businesses must demonstrate that solvency and safety requirements are adhered to through audits and inspections. Large government brings more regulations and more complex regulations. Simple laws require simple means of either compliance or avoidance while complex laws require more complex means. There are so many federal regulations in the developed countries that one person could not possibly read them in his or her entire life. There is a vicious regulatory cycle. Regulations are enacted. Someone finds and exploits a loophole. Further regulations are created to close the loophole. Again, someone finds and exploits another loophole.

People make up the government and people are not perfect. Laws and regulations, therefore, will never be perfect. The issue of interpretation arises. Two people can read the same text yet reach different conclusions. These two people have different backgrounds, education, and work experience. People also place filters over text, actively seeking or excluding meanings that may or may not fit their paradigms. More regulations mean more time and energy spent writing, understanding, clarifying, and rewriting regulations.

Selective enforcement presents another issue. Government employees and representatives have a finite amount of time to address compliance and enforcement. Situations of questionable compliance may emerge, warranting detailed auditing or enforcement actions. Government employees must allocate limited time and "pick their fights." Some entities may escape examination while others are heavily scrutinized. Choosing which entity to "pester" may be driven by consumer complaints or political contributions. "You can pay me and I will leave. Otherwise, I will find something to your detriment" seems to be the prevailing attitude of bureaucrats in many countries in 2020. The fear of retaliation deters people from reporting corruption to higher authorities.

There is a saying in one country that "the complexity and severity of our laws are made tolerable by a lack of enforcement."

Another cost of compliance is inadvertent non-compliance. If laws and regulations are elaborate and arcane, one government department may permit an activity that a different department prohibits. For example, an agency that issues business licenses grants one to a company that installs tinted windows. However, building codes and traffic laws prohibit tinted windows in certain structures or vehicles. The business owner does not know of these prohibitions and has installed tinted windows for several years. Upon discovery, the business is fined and forced to perform restitution for all clients who received the windows outside of the constraints of the law. This economic activity is pure waste, caused by ignorance of the law.

How does society control the government?

Government is made up of people, and people act in their own best interests. Holding a government position allows a person to have power, the power to dictate the actions of others and the power to increase one's wealth. The higher one ascends in the government, the more influence and wealth this person amasses. Historically, people in government positions had parents who also held government positions. Ancient Egypt not only had royalty but governmental positions that evolved from a system based on merit to a system based on inheritance. India developed a caste system to maintain political order. Seats in the Roman Senate became inherited positions of power. England has the House of Lords. In 2020, the United States of America, Russia, China, and Germany all have political dynasties.

What made George Washington a great man? He saw the dangers of political power and although he was tempted to serve as President of the United States for as long as he lived, he relinquished office after two terms. He understood that power corrupts. He understood that the role of leadership was that of a servant to the people. During his tenure, he put the interests of the country first.

The government can be controlled, but it must be controlled by principled people like George Washington.

If a society wants to control the size and power of its government, it must have some measure of the size of government and have incentives to encourage people in government to control themselves.

There may be separate governmental organizations within a country. There may be regional, city, or school governments separate from the federal, or highest level, of government. In this discussion, the federal government is at the top of the hierarchy with the authority to impose requirements on the lower levels, but not vice versa. If society is organized so that lower governmental levels are completely autonomous, then the discussion herein for the federal government applies to them as well.

To control the size of the federal government, one needs to measure government size and wages. The size of the government can be measured by its share of GDP. Wages can be measured in various ways. One possibility is the total government payroll divided by the number of civil servants versus total private-sector wages (as determined from the federal income tax system) divided by the number of workers (from the federal income tax system). Retirees, dependents, non-contributors, and earnings above a certain threshold must be excluded.

The following is a possible methodology to set and adjust government wages. Countless other formulas and factors could be used. The ultimate methodology should be the simplest among viable alternatives. It should be unbiased and not subject to manipulation or interpretation. To develop this specific measure to control the size of government, first compare the salaries of government workers to salaries from the private sector. Then compare the ratio to a benchmark calculated from the government's share of GDP. The specific calculation is shown to give a detailed blueprint.

Define *r* as the ratio of the average government worker's wage to the average private-sector worker's wage, the averages calculated as described in the previous paragraphs. Let *j* and *k* be arbitrary constants, defined by law or regulation. Then look at *j* X (1 – Government % of GDP)^*k* = s (X is multiplied by and ^ is raised to the power of). *k* needs to be greater than or equal to 1.

If *s* is greater than *r*, then government wages must be reduced. Government wage adjustments would be more palatable through the implementation of civil service wage withholding, which would be released after the measurements are made. This gives the appearance of operating a bonus system.

Now give values to the variables in the equation in the simple example. If *j* = 1.05 and *k* = 1.01 and the government's share of GDP is 15%, then *s*, the government wage index, would be 89.1%. This means that civil service workers' pay and benefits would be no more than 89.1% of the private sector average wage. Now assume that the government expands its portion of GDP to 20%, either by government growth or through an economic contraction. The revised government wage index is 83.8%. Civil servants experience a 6% overall pay cut.

There are several important features of a defined and controlled federal government salary system.

First, civil servants should make less than private citizens. Civil service pay should be sufficient to attract quality workers and obviate the need or desire for graft and corruption. The remuneration should not be so high as to foster dynasties at any level. In our example, the civil servant was earning 89% as much as an employee in the private sector. A salary and benefits package at this level would assuredly meet the criteria given in the first three sentences.

Second, a government wage index level should reflect the risk of unemployment. Government jobs have very little risk of loss of employment. Private sector jobs are subject to elimination through technological changes, company buyouts, or competitive pressures. Private sector workers may face periods of unemployment. The costs of re-education or training are not only direct but also manifest as lost wages.

Third, there is an incentive to hold down the size of the government. The inverse relationship between government size and remuneration introduces the desire for efficiency. Although the government wage index level is calculated for the government as a whole, actual salary adjustments could and should be made by department. One wants to avoid a situation where the government as a whole has not met the government wage index due to one department's immense hiring and spending. All other departments should not be punished as severely, if at all.

Fourth, there is an incentive to grow the economy. The government's desire for efficiency is similar to the private sector's desire for efficiency. Private corporations increase earnings by growth and by reducing costs. Private sector growth increases the size of GDP. If the government's share of GDP stays constant, then it has grown as well. Government grows with the economy, not by appropriating parts of the private sector. The government grows by making the pie larger, so to speak, not by taking a bigger piece of the pie.

If government expenditures grew at a slower rate than the general economy, then the government wage index would rise, and civil servants would receive pay increases above the rate experienced in the general economy. The number of civil servants would necessarily need to decrease.

Fifth, all government department expenditures would be subject to GDP growth constraints and the wage indexing methodology. Government spending needs to be controlled. Salaries are only a part of an overall or departmental budget. Other expenses such as travel, supplies, and rent are material components of departmental budgets. The "spend it or lose it" mentality would be replaced by "what we don't spend will be added to our bonuses" mindset.

Sixth, in addition to a wage index to define and control government wages, a defined scale of pay grades with maximums and minimums for each grade must be established. Also, there must be a limit on the ratio of the highest grade to the lowest grade to keep government salaries relatively flat by grade. In addition, reasonable targets for the number of civil servants in each pay grade must be set. The targets should resemble a pyramid, not a cube.

These are proposed measures and controls placed at the federal level. In many countries, there are other levels or sectors of government. These might include schools, universities, cities, or some other semi-autonomous political divisions.

Local governments, in theory, are more responsive to local needs and less susceptible to graft and corruption. In practice, this is not always the case.

A variety of tools can be used to keep local governments under control. The federal government can impose a Fair Distribution Tax, similar to one on corporations. The taxable base can be anything as long as it is defined by law. The federal government can impose pay grade requirements similar to the federal constraints, namely maximum to minimum ratios, and percentage of civil servants in each grade. The federal government may give local governments the option of compliance or paying a federal tax.

Finally, one very effective way to ensure that legislators and civil service executives perform responsible stewardship is to subject them to rigorous and independent financial scrutiny, imposing upon them an excise tax if they have enriched themselves financially at the expense of their constituents. The excise tax rate needs to be greater than 100%.

THE MIDDLE CLASS AND HEALTH CARE

Health care needs a section of the manifesto because of its size and importance to society. In developed countries, it accounts for 15% of GDP, with ample room to grow. In 2020, all developed countries have some type of socialized medicine. They are already experiencing the adverse consequences.

Many politicians have tried to sell socialized medicine by the following argument: Utilities such as water have a single provider, and it is run very well. The government can do the same with health care.

This is of course pure deceit. Utilities are a good, health care is a service. Utilities are easily quantified. Health care is not, nor can it be. Utilities are uniform – the water in Asia is similar to the water in Africa. Health care services are complex and adjusted to patients' needs. Also, like every other industry, when utilities are forced to compete, prices decrease and innovation increases. This happened in the United States with electricity providers. They share equipment but have different pricing options.

First, consider health care from the perspective of a doctor. To become a doctor, one must endure many years in school and a few years in residency (on the job training). The number of expected working years is less than the average worker in society. A long career may not be an option since upon reaching the age of 60 a doctor could discover that practicing medicine is difficult due to health or stamina reasons. There may be an educational cost, at least the cost of self-maintenance, during the learning process.

A physician risks losing employment due to technological or medical innovations, local supply and demand, steerage from large payors, or other factors. Steerage occurs when a large payor contracts with a fraction of the available medical providers in an area (limited network) and covers its members or insureds only for medical services received from the network. An individual physician may experience a sudden, dramatic patient base reduction if he or she is excluded from the network. An important "other factor" is the risk of contracting a debilitating or terminal disease. Physicians and nurses are at a greater risk than the general population of contracting diseases. They may become too sick to work or may not wish to expose their healthy patients to disease through physical contact. The risk of losing employment from all these sources needs to be reflected by increased salary.

Society needs to decide if it wants the best and brightest people in the medical profession. To attract the best and brightest, not only must the physician's expected salary substantially exceed the average worker's salary or wage, the physician must be encouraged to put the patient's welfare first. This means a physician must have a great level of independence.

Society must decide how its physicians should participate in the economy. One possibility is to position physicians in the upper-middle class by structuring a completely privatized medical profession. Another possibility is for physicians to be middle-class civil servants employed by a government-run health care system.

Of course, both structures can be present in a society. Each would have its own patient base.

A physician in a privatized system has the same opportunities for success or failure as the rest of society. Opportunities include building a private practice, joining a group of physicians, or working as an employee of a hospital, health maintenance organization, or government. Society is heterogeneous and physicians are no exception. Offered freedom of choice, physicians will fill every employment niche, depending on individual circumstances, market availability or saturation, and personal preferences. Building a private practice usually entails very lean years at the outset, sometimes requiring an outside source of income for self-maintenance. Also, some physicians may greatly prefer to live in a rural area, in the mountains, by a beach, or where their parents reside. A new physician must consider how many similar physicians and potential patients live in a geographic area. A doctor opening a new practice often will choose a location where patients must wait a long time to see a doctor. Patient wait times are optimized when both doctor and patient can choose their geographic location and patients can choose their doctors.

Opportunities for physicians in a privatized system also include investing in clinics, labs, or ancillary service providers. This may present a conflict of interest but any prudent person invests in familiar enterprises.

In a socialized system, the physician is assigned his or her type of practice and geographic area. In the Union of Soviet Socialistic Republics, this was the norm. Doctors did not have a choice of geographical location and the unfortunate ones who were not politically connected ended up in some undesirable locations, far from family.

In a socialized system, the government decides a medical school graduate's area of practice based on perceived need. A physician may be forced to practice an area of medicine in which he or she has no interest. Patients ultimately suffer. On the positive side, doctors face almost no possibility of unemployment. Because there is no competition among doctors, there is little incentive to adopt innovations. Doctors are people. They think, feel, behave, and reason just like other normal, rational people in society. They will follow financial incentives. Doctors who are given a salary will see fewer patients a day compared to doctors paid per patient visit. Macro-economically speaking, productivity in the medical sector is lower under a socialized system.

One also sees reduced productivity in capitated arrangements - where a doctor receives a monthly payment from the payor (whether the payor is the government or an insurance company) for each person assigned to him or her. The physician must treat each patient at no additional charge (except for a fixed nominal copayment in some cases). The sickest patients compensate the capitated doctor the least when translated to an hourly basis. Emergency room usage by patients of capitated doctors is greater than that of fee-for-service doctors. The reason is the physician-patient relationship is not as strong. Capitated doctors have an incentive to ration care and their sicker patients are left untreated. Their conditions worsen until acute care becomes necessary.

In socialized medicine, the government specifies the treatment, given the diagnosis. Doctors must follow government treatment protocols. There is little customization or accommodation of the patient's desires. Canada in 2020 uses this kind of system as part of its national health care bureaucracy, mandating the hierarchy of treatments for most diagnoses. For example, a doctor treats a patient for a foot infection. He or she knows from clinical experience which antibiotic is most effective against foot bacteria. This antibiotic ranks fourth on a list from the mandated treatment plan. He or she must first prescribe the other three antibiotics and watch the patient worsen before finally curing the patient with the preferred antibiotic.

Diagnostic procedures are rationed. Even if an MRI could be useful, unless the diagnosis is sufficiently severe, a doctor cannot order it. Conversely, if the diagnosis is severe enough to qualify for an MRI, the doctor is obligated to order one despite knowing the condition and treatment of the malady. Here, the doctor is compensated an additional amount for reviewing the test results.

From the perspective of the doctor, a private system is by far the more desirable.

Because patients have a choice of providers in a privatized system, a physician is incented to build a strong doctor-patient relationship and to provide treatment according to the patient's expectations. Some patients fear potent drugs, preferring holistic remedies or a diet regimen. Some patients want a quick solution even if it involves surgery. Others can tolerate discomfort.

In 2020 and beyond, patients can access all kinds of information on the Internet. They use the Internet to self-diagnose and find appropriate medical providers. All patients benefit collectively from free choice. When someone has a medical problem, the person visits his or her regular doctor, usually a general practitioner, for treatment or a referral to a specialist. He or she also asks family, friends, and neighbors for recommendations. The person also searches the Internet for reviews, procedures, and prices. Generally, a full waiting room is a good sign when searching for a physician.

Mathematically, a free choice system is a collection of individual decision-makers. Each has imperfect information and each has a defined medical condition among a finite list of possibilities. If the decision-maker has an unfavorable experience with a provider, he will shop for a new provider. If he has a favorable experience, he will revisit the provider. Through trial and error, individual decision-makers gravitate to the best providers. They also improve the information base by adding their positive or negative experiences. New decision-makers will rely on the information base, steering themselves to the best providers more often and more quickly.

Less capable providers will be forced to charge less or join a network with a captive patient pool. This is precisely what happens in the United States. Insurance plans recruit physicians based on willingness to accept low fees, throwing quality of care out the window.

Health care systems run by governments take one of two forms. If there is an established private system, the government offers providers in the system insultingly low fees or capitations to treat targeted members of society eligible for free or subsidized government coverage. The providers agreeing to the terms are the most desperate and least qualified. In the second system, providers become civil servants. This model is adopted when no competing private system exists or, as in the case of the military, when a self-contained segment of society is associated in some manner with the government.

Mathematically, a government system is also comprised of individual decision-makers. In this case, if the decision-maker has an unfavorable experience, he must request re-assignment. Unlike the free choice system, the assignment is not made using an information base but rather an availability base. Assignment is made to the provider with the most available capacity. Instead of gravitating to the best providers, patients are at best given random providers and at worst shuffled between the least desirable providers because these providers have the most unused capacity. Since there is no information base and no choice, new entrants cannot benefit from the cumulative experience of the decision-makers.

Socialized medicine is more costly to patients in terms of time and adverse medical outcomes than a privatized system.

Next, examine privatized versus socialized medicine from the point of the payor. The payor may be the individual, the individual utilizing insurance, a third-party payor, or the government. In either system, the payor is part of the decision-making process with the provider and the patient.

The most efficient use of health care occurs when the individual pays his or her own medical costs. In this case, the person ultimately deciding the course of treatment has a financial stake in his or her future health. Most medical costs occur in the first and last years of life. A person at the end of life has the option to undergo expensive treatment, giving his or her accumulated wealth to the medical system. A second option is to accept death with as little pain as possible, foregoing the possibility of a cure. Often, one chooses something in between these extremes.

When choosing a course of treatment, the individual must weigh whether to give part of his accumulated wealth to the medical system or his heirs (for whom he presumably cares). The decision hinges on treatment costs versus individual net worth. A person with a 50 million unit net worth may opt for a treatment costing 1 million units while another with a 2 million unit net worth would think twice. The person with a 100,000 unit net worth would not have the expensive treatment as an option. Factors that are part of the treatment decision are the post-treatment costs and eventual quality of life. If one expects to be confined to a bed in a nursing home for months if not years, even a wealthy person would balk at the cost versus quality. While these considerations might suffice for the elderly, a pure individual payor system is inappropriate for newborns.

The term "anti-selection" describes the behavior of a person acting in his or her own best interests in an insurance or risk-taking setting. A person seeking insurance knows more about his or her circumstances than an insurance company. One needing medical treatment will buy health insurance or ensure payment for existing insurance. An individual blessed with good health may wish to apply his or her money to investments, allowing insurance coverage to lapse.

Also with anti-selection, a person plagued by a medical condition will seek out the most comprehensive insurance plan while avoiding coverage with high deductibles and other cost-sharing requirements. A healthy, responsible individual would opt to cover an unforeseen catastrophe caused by accident or sickness. One may see the effects when health insurance plans are placed side-by-side for a price comparison. The plan with richer benefits is more expensive than the lesser plan due to the cost of benefits and the percentage of the population selecting the plans.

For example, consider a population in which 80% use 90 units of medical care and 20% use 140 units.

Table 47: Medical Care Used		
Percentage of Population	Medical Care Used	Weighted Medical Care Used (col 1 X col 2)
80%	90	72
20%	140	28
100%		100

If this population could enroll in only one insurance plan covering 90% of medical costs, the premium would be 90% times 100 (weighted medical care used) = 90. If the only plan available to them covered 75% of medical costs, the premium would be 75.

Table 48: Premium Calculation – Only One Plan Covering 90% of Medical Costs Offered		
Weighted Medical Care	100	Line 3, Col 3 from Table 47
Percentage of Population	100%	Line 3, Col 1 from Table 47
Percentage of Medical Costs Covered	90%	
Premium Rate (line 1 / line 2 X line 3)	90	

Table 49: Premium Calculation – Only One Plan Covering 75% of Medical Costs Offered		
Weighted Medical Care	100	Line 3, Col 3 from Table 47
Percentage of Population	100%	Line 3, Col 1 from Table 47
Percentage of Medical Costs Covered	75%	
Premium Rate (line 1 / line 2 X line 3)	75	

If the population had a choice between the two insurance plans, one might see that from the portion of the population with a 90 unit medical usage (80% of the total), 10% would choose the 90% plan and 70% would choose the 75% plan. Healthier people would shop to save money if possible. From the portion of the population with medical problems, 15% would choose the 90% plan and 5% would choose the 75% plan.

Table 50: Distribution of Medical Risks and Plans Chosen			
	Percentage of Population	Medical Care Used	Weighted Medical Care Used (col 1 X col 2)
90% Plan			
	10%	90	9
	15%	140	21
	25%		30
75% Plan			
	70%	90	63
	5%	140	7
	75%		70

Premium Calculation for 90% Plan – Individual has a choice of two plans

Table 51: Premium Calculation for 90% Plan – Individual has a Choice of Two Plans		
Weighted Medical Care	30	Line 3, Col 4 from Table 50
Percentage of Population	25%	Line 3, Col 1 from Table 50
Percentage of Medical Costs Covered	90%	
Premium Rate (line 1 / line 2 X line 3)	108	

Table 52: Premium Calculation for 75% Plan – Individual has a Choice of Two Plans		
Weighted Medical Care	70	Line 6, Col 4 from Table 50
Percentage of Population	75%	Line 6, Col 1 from Table 50
Percentage of Medical Costs Covered	75%	
Premium Rate (line 1 / line 2 X line 3)	70	

Several points are worth noting from the simple example.

First, the ratio of the premium rates is not the same as the percentage of medical costs covered. The premium rates are 108/70=1.54, while the benefits are 90/75=1.2.

Second, people do not buy insurance (or any product) based on expected values but rather based on something called a "utility function." The utility function is a mathematical way to handle perceived value, incorporating intangibles such as enjoyment, urgency, or fear. People are afraid of losing a large and important possession, such as their house or health, and will pay an unreasonable sum of money to protect themselves. They do not make a statistical calculation and do not simply walk away from a situation in which all companies offering protection charge unreasonable rates. Homeowners' insurance provides an easy illustration. The typical annual premium is 1% of the value of the house. This is equivalent to one house in a hundred destroyed every year. This is of course absurd.

Third, actual premiums in reality for both plans are higher than simply the expected costs. Actual premiums contain a margin for administration, taxes, compliance, marketing costs, and profit.

In another simple example, consider three plans. The first is a comprehensive plan that pays 95% of all costs. The second is a hospitalization-only plan. Hospitalization expenses typically comprise 40% of total medical costs. The third is a high-deductible plan only paying expenses exceeding a typical annual salary. The frequency of these expenses is low but the cost per expense is high. These kinds of expenses typically comprise 5% of total medical expenses.

The table below shows pricing and provision for expenses for the three plans.

Table 53: Premium to Cover Medical Expenses for Three Types of Coverage

	Most Costs Covered	Certain Costs Covered	Catastrophic Costs Covered
Underlying Total Medical Costs	100	100	100
Expected Medical Costs Insured as Percentage of Total	95%	40%	5%
Number of People in Sample	10,000	10,000	10,000
Number of People Incurring the Medical Cost	9,990	1,600	4
Standard Deviation in Medical Costs	0.03	0.92	1.00
Expected Cost plus Full Standard Deviation	95.03	40.92	6.00
Percentage of Premium for Admin. Expenses	20%	30%	45%
Final Total Premium	118.79	58.45	10.91
Amount of Premium for Admin. Expenses	23.76	17.54	4.91

In the middle column, which covers hospital costs, 16% of people account for 40% of total costs. Hospital costs are typically large. Similarly, for the catastrophic plan, 0.04% of the people are responsible for 5% of total costs.

The Standard Deviation in Costs is calculated by a simple formula: $(p(1-p)/n)^0.5$, where p is the number of people incurring the cost divided by the number of people in the sample, and n is the number of people in the sample.

The Final Total Premium is the Expected Cost plus Full Standard Deviation divided by (1 minus Percentage of Premium for Administrative Expenses).

The Amount of Premium for Administrative Expenses is the Final Total Premium less the Expected Cost plus Full Standard Deviation.

The following table shows the cost of medical care to consumers:

Table 54: Cost to the Consumer of Medical Care with Health Insurance for Three Types of Coverage

	Most Costs Covered	Certain Costs Covered	Catastrophic Costs Covered
Underlying Total Costs	100	100	100
Expected Costs Insured	95	40	5
Expected Costs Borne by Consumer	5	60	95
Final Premium	118.79	58.45	10.91
Premium plus Medical Costs Borne by Consumer	123.79	118.45	105.91

Several points are worth noting.

First, the most adverse financial impact on the middle class comes from the most comprehensive coverage. This is because the insurer takes an extra percentage on top of every medical service. The insurer needs the fee for contracting, processing, financial reporting, compliance, and marketing. It must maintain some relationship with every provider or a large subset of providers. It is also in business to earn a profit or contribute to surplus.

Second, the insurer's administrative charge for the hospital-only plan is a larger percentage of the premium than the comprehensive plan but the total dollar burden to the consumer is less. In this instance, the insurer must only administer claims for 16% of the population, and only have contracts with a portion of the medical community.

Third, the lowest burden on the middle class is when insurance is used to cover catastrophic losses. The premium is over twice the expected cost but the consumer bases the decision to buy on a utility function. The consumer's total medical expenditures are only 6% above actual costs. In this instance, the insurer does not require contracts with providers and only handles a relatively small number of large claims.

Extreme anti-selection happens when a person has a known medical problem. He or she will seek out the most comprehensive coverage attainable. If this person already carries insurance, he will make sure to keep it while shopping for better coverage. If the person has no insurance, he or she will try to somehow get covered. Because this is a behavior event and not a statistical event, insurers cannot blindly assume risks such as these and hope to stay in business. Sometimes people make poor decisions, like foregoing needed protection. They are adults and understand that poor decisions have financial consequences.

For newborns, and the very young, health insurance dynamics are different. The unborn do not make decisions. The only anti-selection occurs when a problem is diagnosed before birth, a rare event not subject to personal control or mitigation. There are instances when the mother abuses drugs or other substances. The fetus suffers the adverse impacts but does not control these actions.

So newborns and the very young are a fairly homogeneous population with defined expected costs. The medical costs for newborns are primarily the costs of delivery. The vast majority are normal deliveries, a known percentage will have minor complications, and a small percentage will have major complications. The frequencies and amounts can be quantified and the resulting cost can be assessed to the affected population. The affected population might be narrowly defined as expectant mothers or broadly defined as the population in general.

The post-delivery medical costs for the first five years of life are modest. These usually entail well-child assessments and vaccinations. Some diseases like asthma or allergies become manifest at these ages. The expected costs are defined and there is no anti-selection. Like deliveries, the costs of early childhood medical care can be assessed to the affected population.

Also, unlike the elderly, parents of newborns are usually not as economically well off as the population in general. Because parents are young, they have not had time to accumulate assets. So, a pure fee-for-service system is not appropriate for newborns. A certain percentage of newborns have major complications and require expensive care but most will recover and become economically productive. The decision to treat must not be a short term decision based exclusively on financial considerations.

If the payor is the patient carrying insurance, then a contract, which must follow applicable laws, defines the decision to treat. The consumer chooses an insurer much like he or she shops for any product or service. He or she researches company reputation, especially in the area of consumer complaints. Information may be available through government licensing departments or third-party quality rating bureaus.

Usually, one would expect that high medical costs would be covered because that is the fundamental purpose of insurance. The insurance company has the right to determine if there was a pre-existing condition, but only within a defined and limited time period. One creative way to mitigate medical costs through insurance would be for the insurance company to estimate, especially in terminal cases, the costs of intensive and comprehensive treatment to the costs of palliative care over the expected remaining life of the insured. Then, to incent the patient to accept palliative care, the insurer would offer the patient a sum of money representing a percentage of the estimated difference in cost between comprehensive treatment and palliative treatment. The patient could choose the money and palliative care, increasing his or her estate for the enjoyment of the heirs, or opt for the more expensive treatment instead.

One would expect that newborns would be covered under a more comprehensive and universal system, at least for the majority of hospital and physician delivery costs.

If the payor is a third party, conflicting goals and priorities become manifest. The consumer wants the best medical care possible regardless of cost. The payor wants the least expensive delivery method. Quality is not important, outcomes are not important, the patient's life is not important. Any financial reward inures to the payor. The consumer has no incentive to contain spending on health care.

A third-party payor system has given rise to various forms of rationing. The first is a restricted network of health care providers. The criterion for participation in the network is usually consenting to a low fee schedule. The lower the fee schedule, the fewer doctors who accept it. Those who do are usually less desirable.

The second is a determined treatment plan dictated by the payor. Only the least expensive and least effective treatment regimen and prescription drugs will be approved and paid for. Doctors must follow a treatment plan in coordination with nurses employed by the payor.

The third is a gatekeeper mechanism. All treatment must be reviewed and approved by a primary care doctor, who may try to treat the condition personally first. Referrals to a specialist take time. Effective treatment is at best deferred and at worst withheld.

The payor has a financial incentive to withhold necessary care even if denial ultimately leads to more expensive care. If the consumer participates in insurance through employment or other transitory situations, the likelihood arises that, with normal employee or other turnover, a person needing medical care will eventually become someone else's problem. Or if the payor is a government agency, the patient may become the responsibility of a program sponsored by a different government entity. In the best possible scenario, the patient is left untreated and dies.

If the payor is the government, then not only do all the characteristics of the third-party payor situation apply, but additional challenges emerge as well. If the government is the only payor, it can pick and choose winners and losers within the system.

Government is best when it is the arbiter between the big guy and the little guy. The government can effectively create and enforce a level playing field. But when the government has a financial stake in the outcome, it becomes the big guy with the little guy having no recourse.

If the government picks winners and losers in a game in which it has a financial interest, it somehow always wins. Most developed countries with elected representative governments focus on the short term. Next year's budget is more important than the budget in ten years because by then it most likely will be someone else's problem.

Therefore, it is also in the government's interest to defer or withhold costly medical treatment.

The government budget is susceptible to deductible leveraging. The simple example below illustrates the phenomenon. Three government programs cover combined services costing 1,000 units in total. These services would cost 1,000 units in the presence or absence of government as a payor. The first government program pays for all the costs. The second pays for all the costs except 50 units, which the citizen must pay. The third program covers 600 units and the citizen must pay 400 units. In each case, the citizen pays a deductible. In other words, the citizen pays first until reaching a pre-defined limit before the government pays.

In Year 2, the underlying costs increase by 5%. The increase may be due to the price per service, number of services performed, intensity of services, or pent up demand of services previously withheld. In Year 2, the citizen's deductible has not changed, perhaps due to an elected government's reluctance to force citizens to pay more for coverage. Many government programs have indices that automatically increase cost-sharing. However, these indices may not capture all changes in the underlying economy. For example, they may capture a price increase on a basket of services but not a change in the composition of that basket. In our simple example, the cost-sharing indexed formula shows no change.

Table 55: Examples showing the Effect of Deductible Leveraging on Government Program Costs			
Year 1	Government Program #1	Government Program #2	Government Program #3
Underlying Cost of Services	1,000	1,000	1,000
Citizen's Deductible	0	50	400
Government's Cost	1,000	950	600
Year 2			
Percentage Increase in Cost of Services	5%	5%	5%
Underlying Cost of Services	1,050	1,050	1,050
Citizen's Deductible	0	50	400
Government's Cost	1,050	1,000	650
Increase in Government Expenditures	(1,050-1,000)/1,000 = 5%	(1,000-950)/950 = 5.26%	(650-600)/600 = 8.33%

The Increase in Government Expenditures is the Year 2 Government's Cost less Year 1 Government's Cost, divided by the Year 1 Government's Cost.

If there is consumer cost-sharing and the consumers' deductibles do not increase, then the government experiences a budget increase exceeding GDP growth for that sector.

The higher the consumer sharing as a percentage of costs, the larger the budget increase. In the real world, prescription drugs usually have a high level of consumer cost-sharing, sometimes as much as 40% to 60% of the prescription drug costs. While drug costs may appear to be spiraling out of control, these increases are simply deductible (or cost-sharing) leveraging.

If the government is the payor, its measured costs and resulting expenditures will very likely exceed GDP growth. This result would cause political concern.

THE MIDDLE CLASS AND RELIGION

Karl Marx was an atheist and held people with religious beliefs in low regard. He advocated for the eradication of religion because socialism and religion are incompatible.

Mankind has held some religious belief system from time immemorial. Among various religions, explanations regarding creation, descriptions of miracles, or theories surrounding the afterlife seem incredulous to many. However, there is one important life experience that atheists and scientists cannot explain:

Consciousness.

Consciousness exists although it cannot be isolated or measured. No scientific hypotheses or repeatable experiments explain the nature and composition of consciousness. There is an unmistakable link between life and consciousness. There is also a link between sensory perception and consciousness.

We each experience the world through our senses. Part of the experience is interacting with others. Interaction seems to be a basic human need. Through interaction, we develop empathy and sympathy. We understand that other people also have consciousness with similar feelings, desires, and goals as ours. We also learn that not all interactions between people are positive.

Part of our conscious experience is knowing right from wrong. Right and Wrong form the basis of a society's morals. There are rewards for good behavior and punishment for bad behavior. More fundamentally, our conscious being senses the difference between Right and Wrong.

One basic purpose of religion is to define right and wrong. God, far superior in wisdom to any creature, charged humans with this determination. Divinely inspired prophets preached and recorded moral parameters and guidelines for humans to follow. During ancient times, people readily accepted these moral rules for two reasons: First, rules were codified in a miraculous or inspired manner. Tablets were created overnight from blank stone, with reliable witnesses attesting to the event. Second, the rules had a calming effect on people. These rules were complete, relatively simple to understand, and consistent with a person's innate notions of what should be right and wrong.

Governing and interacting with people is much easier when they have a moral compass. The more resolute people's convictions are, the more efficient society is. Less law enforcement is needed. If people are governed by "do unto others as you would have them do unto you," then society will not need reams of pages of laws. If people live in a nation that values their families, then they will sacrifice themselves to protect that nation.

Christian doctrine is well suited as a basis for an orderly, compassionate, and just society. These essential characteristics of Christianity enabled the faith to spread and, once adopted, become cherished and difficult to remove or replace.

First, there is a God who is actually a Trinity, one God with three coeternal hypostases, "one God in three Divine Persons," each with His separate function and purpose.

Jesus Christ is one-third of the Trinity. He came to mortal Earth for several reasons. One was to prove the existence of an afterlife. The second was to lay out the New Testament or Covenant, which states that God will forgive sin if one sincerely repents and welcome those who truly want a relationship with Him. The third was to teach and reinforce proper thought and behavior for a civil society – to explain good and evil. The fourth was to perform very public miracles, including His death by crucifixion and His subsequent resurrection. The fifth was to evangelize the faith by encouraging the spreading of the New Testament and supporting ministry.

The Ten Commandments from the Old Testament are still in effect.

The Golden Rule, as stated by Christ, is "Do to others as you would have them do to you" (Matthew 7:12; Luke 6:31). This is the cornerstone of human interaction.

"As you did it to one of the least of my brothers, you did it to me" (Matthew 25:40) forms the basis of how a person is ultimately viewed and judged by God.

Once a person has embraced Christianity and is accepted by the grace of God, that person is obliged to demonstrate his faith by his deeds. He or she must care about others, help strangers in need, volunteer at church, be encouraging, tithe, study the Bible, read and listen to sermons, and write or record thoughts and prayers.

Finally, living a Christian life does not mean that one allows himself or herself to be "treated like a doormat." Nor does one have to accept being taken advantage of by others. One is not required to put the welfare of others ahead of one's own. At the time of Jesus, around 20% of the Roman population were slaves. A slave's obedience and a slave owner's responsibility are addressed in both the Old and New Testaments. Both the slave and owner could be Christian. The most unfair economic relationship could still be guided by the Golden Rule.

Christianity grew because of its doctrines and the steadfastness of its adherents. People chose to be thrown to the lions rather than renounce their faith. They had personally witnessed Christ's crucifixion and resurrection or knew someone or someone's ancestor who had. The fear of God was much more intense than the fear of man.

Romans managed society in a generally orderly way, and religion was no exception. In 325, the Roman Emperor Constantine convened the First Council of Nicaea. It was a gathering of religious scholars to standardize Christian doctrine, religious observances, and the Bible. They were tasked with deciding which texts among those in use by a myriad of Christian sects were the inspired Word of God and should be assembled in the standardized Bible. There was considerable review, thought, prayer, and discussion in a collective effort spanning a great many years. In the year 367, the Bishop of Alexandria announced that agreement on the content and order of the books of the Bible had been achieved. By 382, when the Latin translation of the Bible began, the standard version was firmly established. In the construction of the Bible, many texts in use were reviewed and considered unsuitable due to their various conflicts with accepted doctrine. Some discarded texts survived into the 21st century and were occasionally "discovered" in remote locations. The news media has reported these discoveries as something which had been overlooked and could potentially change some of Christian doctrine. Anyone familiar with history knows that this reporting is complete nonsense.

Once Christianity became the official religion of the Roman Empire in 380, it was never supplanted. Only with the Muslim conquest of Roman territory was Christianity forcibly replaced. Pockets of Christians remain in the Muslim world, despite extreme persecution.

Christianity spread throughout Europe. The Catholic Church was the religion of choice in Western Europe while the Eastern Orthodox Church (officially known as the Orthodox Catholic Church) was followed in Eastern Europe. Kings, royalty, and nobility recognized the power and opportunity in the church. When leaders of society adopted Christianity, they made it the official religion of their realms. Whichever denomination was decreed as the official religion became the beneficiary of religious tax revenues. Taxes were collected from all subjects to support the chosen denomination. This was not necessarily good or bad but a fact of life.

Throughout the Middle Ages, church and state were very closely tied. Both offered opportunities for wealth and power. High-ranking nobility and high-ranking clergy often came from the same families. If a nobleman had three sons, only the eldest could inherit the title and estate. The other two often were given positions in the church. Also, a separate hierarchical establishment existed within the church. Priests inherited their positions of wealth and power from their fathers.

The accumulation of wealth and worldliness within the echelons of the Catholic Church was addressed in the Lateran Councils of 1123 and 1139. The Catholic Church could not fix all of societies' problems, but they could remedy the nepotism and concentration of wealth within the Church. The solution was to forbid the clergy from marrying. This meant they would have no heirs and could focus on their ministries and service to others.

The Eastern Orthodox Church did not seem to have this problem to this extent, so marriage and families have been the way of life for its clergy.

In Western Europe during the early 1500s, the Christian Church began to fracture. First Martin Luther in 1517 wrote the "Ninety-Five Theses." The Anglican Church arose in England when Parliament enacted the Act of Supremacy in 1534. Thereafter, several other Protestant denominations and sects were also founded. Nations continued the practice of maintaining an official religion supported by taxation. Individuals who were members of a sect other than the official religion essentially had to tithe to the official religion as well to as their chosen religion.

In the 1600s, Catholicism was introduced to Central and South America. At the time, many New World indigenous cultures practiced religions involving child sacrifice. Imagine a young parent with a five-year-old child. Would he or she choose a religion espousing "Allow little children to come unto me, for such is the kingdom of God" (Matthew 19:14) or a religion that maintained "We seem to be having dry weather. A few child sacrifices are in order ... and your child will have the honor"? Funny how the priests' children were never quite honorable enough, though.

In the 1600s, a variety of Christian denominations migrated to North America. Each community had a dominant denomination, which may have been associated with its colony's charter from the Crown. People were excited about congregating and worshiping as they wished.

In the 1730s and 1740s, North American colonies experienced a period of evangelical revivals called the First Great Awakening. Evangelists preached personal morality, piety, and dedication. They stressed that people should adhere to the teachings of Jesus and should welcome the Holy Spirit into their hearts. It was a time when virtuous values were instilled into the colonists. It was the time in which the founders of the United States of America were born. The First Great Awakening had a profound influence on the founders' values, their tolerance, and their respect and value of other people.

The founding of the United States of America was a unique event in history. The best and brightest people came together to create a set of rules for a new nation. The founders were not only highly educated but also had strong moral compasses. Every meeting began with a prayer. In 1787, the Constitution was completed. Due to concerns regarding the federal government's power, and potential abuse thereof, a Bill of Rights was ratified in 1791 guaranteeing citizens specific personal freedoms and rights.

The Bill of Rights contains the following two provisions of note: The First Amendment forbids the establishment of a national religion. This is the basis of the separation of church and state. The purpose of this wording was to address the practice found in Europe of adopting official national religions supported by taxation. In the United States, there was to be no national religion. From the influence of the First Great Awakening, which encompassed and included all denominations, every citizen of the United States had the right to worship as he chose, and all religions had equal status.

The doctrine of separation of church and state never meant that religion should be excluded from public or government institutions. The justification for establishing public schools was to teach children to read the Bible and public schools used the Bible as a text for over 100 years.

The Fifth Amendment states in part that no person shall be deprived of life, liberty or property without due process of law. Also, private property shall not be taken for public use without just compensation. The founders understood the importance of protecting property. If the fruits of a person's labor or one's inheritance could be arbitrarily confiscated, then that person really owns nothing and has no incentive to create anything.

These are cornerstones to a vibrant middle class. These are two fundamental traits of a civil society.

THE MIDDLE CLASS AND CIVIL SOCIETY

A "civil society" is defined as a nation or community in which members strive to achieve a common good. Members in their hearts truly believe in justice and fairness and have the wisdom to administer these attributes. Members are honest in thought, word, and deed. They have the wisdom to discern deception. They bring things out from the good stored up in their hearts.

When this manifesto refers to civil society it is using this definition, which is closest to the original Greek usage (around 400 BC). The term civil society has been co-opted by a variety of authors to suit a variety of purposes, some of which are deliberate obfuscations.

A civil society has a religious core. As discussed earlier, right and wrong are absolute and unchanging when based on a higher authority. There is an established written document to refer to and interpret if necessary. Statutory laws should be consistent with religious doctrine. This does not mean religious control of the government.

Religion should be used as a guidepost, not a weapon. Priests and other ordained leaders have the right, but not the duty, to publicly admonish secular leaders when their behavior or proposed legislation is contrary to religious teachings and principles. The obligation to abide by and respect religious authorities lies on government and public institutions.

A civil society that loses its religious foundation gradually degenerates. There is no moral compass and society is guided by "might makes right." Whoever has might makes and selectively enforces the "rules." Rules and social norms become arbitrary. Political might is either achieved militarily or by alliances. Young people are indoctrinated to support those in power.

Marx understood the importance of religion. Communism and socialism are antithetical to religion and antithetical to moral and decent behavior. The ideology must be instilled into society gradually and surreptitiously.

A civil society venerates and protects life. To civil society, all life matters. In a civil society, the lowest members are given a measure of love and protection. The lowest members are the unborn. They have no money, no voice, and no ability to vote. They do, however, have their whole future before them. They are also the most innocent of the innocent. Any society that allows abortion, except in rare cases, is not a civil society. Members who support abortion do not truly believe in justice and fairness. They are either dishonest in word and deed or if their beliefs are genuine, very dangerous. These people are egocentric. They cannot be trusted to put the welfare of others ahead of their own. They cannot be trusted to give one iota of consideration to others.

The lives and well-being of animals are also important. Animals should not suffer needlessly. Animals have limited communicative ability but can convey pain or fear. Animals treated with love respond with loyalty and affection. One notices personality differences between simple-minded livestock treated with compassion and those treated with cruelty or indifference. Most of these animals end their lives in an abattoir, where their slaughter should be done as humanely as possible.

PROPERTY RIGHTS IN A CIVIL SOCIETY

A civil society respects property rights – no matter if the property has great value or marginal value. In a civil society, no one would even consider taking something that is not his or her own. If a person leaves his or her watch or phone unattended in a public or semi-private area, he or she should not fear the theft of the property.

A person who steals cannot enjoy the fruits of theft. If one steals another's watch or jewelry, he or she can't wear it. He or she can't have it on public display or have the object fulfill its purpose. Similarly, jewelry inadvertently left in a hotel room does not become the property of the maid or the hotel owner. The value of an item decreases when it is stolen. Attempting to sell forgotten jewelry carries a risk of an encounter with law enforcement. Anyone potentially involved with the sale or resale of misplaced property must exchange the property at a diminished price to account for the risk of forfeiture.

There are certain subcultures with no respect for property rights. People in these subcultures simply take any property that seems the least bit unguarded. Their self-centered justification is "the current owner is not using this. I might as well." This attitude extends to food stored in a pantry, implements in a yard or farm, or even residences. Some will strip the copper wiring from a ranch or unoccupied house for its salvage value or remove used appliances and attempt to sell them. This is doubly destructive. The existing asset, the house, is reduced in value due to the theft. The value of the house without wiring or appliances plus the salvage value of the copper or the value of a used appliance with no warranty is far less than the value of the intact house. Restoring the asset to its original value requires additional funds. This mindset and behavior are destructive to the middle class.

Some people have the audacity to move into an unoccupied house and then act as if they own it. They imagine that they have established what is termed "squatters' rights." Unfortunately, in some instances, legal maneuvers protect or even aid squatters. In Venezuela under the rule of the socialist regime, renters were given title to the houses they occupied. The landlord simply forfeited the property even though he or she had paid for it and was relying on the rent for income.

A property owner has certain rights. The owner may enjoy the property as he or she pleases, improve or modify it, use it as collateral, offer it for rent, buy or sell it, or even destroy it as long as no law is violated or recompense is sought. Only the property owner may do this. Nobody else has these rights, nor should they expect to receive these rights.

Citizenship rights are property rights. A citizen of a country has rights that non-citizens do not. A citizen may vote, own property, work legally, change residences, operate certain vehicles, own a business, remain in the country, get married, bestow citizenship upon his or her children, hold elected office, be protected from extradition, and may have many other rights not listed. Citizens determine the qualifications and processes to be followed for non-citizens to become citizens. No one outside of the country has these rights and should not expect to receive them.

A citizen is entitled to certain government programs. A non-citizen knows or should know that he or she has no such entitlements. A non-citizen should not expect or receive an entitlement.

Citizenship and property rights give the owner defined and exclusive rights to enjoy certain activities. There may be obligations as well, like paying taxes, maintaining a certain aesthetic or functional standard, performing military or community service, not violating laws or having a prison record, serving on a jury, adopting a certain religion, or some other obligation. A non-citizen has not met some or any of these obligations.

Someone without property or citizenship rights cannot assert them. This is equivalent to asserting squatters' rights. Someone who thinks and behaves in this manner is again self-centered and has no regard for his fellow man. Imagine that you own a large house. One day a stranger shows up completely uninvited and moves into one of your bedrooms. The stranger is indignant. He says that you have many rooms, you are not using this room, and this bedroom is better than his current living conditions. You tell him that he is not welcome in your house. He then pays you a fair rent and tells you he is staying.

This illustrates uncontrolled illegal immigration from the viewpoint of the average middle-class citizen. If someone has the right to occupy your home, then it is not really your home. If someone has the right to occupy your country, then it is not really your country. Your citizenship – and its accompanying rights, benefits, and obligations – is meaningless. You have no protection under the law, no recourse through the law, and live in a society where might makes right.

To take our example one step further, the squatter brings ten of his friends into the house. The squatters decide that they no longer want the original homeowner to live there, so they throw him into the street. Now the homeowner must find a weaker person to victimize and becomes a squatter himself. Society has descended into mob rule, its lowest form.

FAIRNESS IN A CIVIL SOCIETY

A civil society demands that members treat others fairly. The notion of "fair" may not be precise, but fair treatment and dealings are characterized by honesty, consistency, and equity. A fair trial means that all parties are heard without prejudice. Issues are decided based upon the facts, not the social or economic status of the individuals involved. The judges or arbiters must put personal interests aside.

When selling a product or performing a service, the product or service must be truthfully described and terms of the transaction must be agreed to in advance. Any substitutions or alterations are prohibited and if made, are justifiable causes for voidance of the transaction. The price of a product or service may vary but only if the variance is rational and transparent. For example, delivering a tractor to a farm 50 kilometers away is more expensive than delivering a tractor 1 kilometer away. The cost of gasoline, transit time, and safety precautions are reasonable considerations.

Is it fair to provide a product or service at a price that varies by a customer's ability to pay? This aligns with Karl Marx's motto: "From each according to his ability, to each according to his needs." In theory, it sounds laudable but to apply the principle in real life is problematic. For example, suppose a retailer sells vacuum cleaners. The price is 50 units for low-income people, 100 units for high-income people, and the government subsidizes the difference. One problem is verifying low income. There will be an incentive to misrepresent. There will be people with variable incomes that rise above and fall below the income threshold. Finally, this practice will launch a resale market. Some poor people will buy vacuum cleaners for 50 units and resell them for 70 units, in effect using the subsidies as a source of income.

Fairness manifests itself in employment. Is it fair for a business owner to keep the lion's share of the income, paying employees such a marginal rate that both spouses have to work to make a living wage? For example, suppose a scientist discovers a cure for a terrible disease afflicting millions. The scientist makes millions, and legitimately so. But what of his or her assistant researchers and lab technicians? Are their contributions worthless?

Take the example one step further. Suppose a wealthy man owned the research facility and operation. He employed the scientist and support staff to develop the vaccine. As a contractual condition of employment, the wealthy man owned all patents and rights related to vaccines developed in his business. There was no guarantee that anything successful would or could be developed. If nothing were developed, the wealthy man would have wasted his money on the research.

The wealthy man spent money, took risks, and it paid off astoundingly well. He then decides to concentrate on the vaccine's production so he terminates the scientist and all research staff. In his opinion, the scientist and researchers were looking for jobs when they found the jobs he gave them and he has no obligation to keep them in his hire.

Several things to consider arise from these examples. First, fairness is not always absolute or obvious. There are situations where, if you asked 100 people to decide what constituted fair treatment, 60 would see it one way while 40 would see it the other. Second, just because someone signs a document does not mean its terms are fair. A potential employee desperately needing work is apt to acquiesce to very unfavorable treatment. Some employers maintain a culture of low pay and high demands. They fully expect their employees to remain only long enough to find another job. The business has a high turnover, which stresses employees. Everyone is treated equally badly.

Fair does not necessarily mean nice. A civil society's concept of fair should include compassion. Developed societies have decided that the practice of putting young children to work is not fair or desirable. Historically, this is a relatively recent reform. Developed societies have provisions for disabled workers and medical treatment for severely disabled children. This demonstrates the veneration and protection of human life. Fair treatment usually depends on a society's economic resources. A poor nation is more apt to adopt a "survival of the fittest" philosophy.

"Do unto others as you would have them do unto you" is a double-edged sword. Suppose a man deliberately murdered a child. His action indicates that he has an active desire to be put to death. Society should accommodate him. Theft of property should be punished with not only full restitution to the victim but should also include a financial penalty. Similarly, violent assaults should be answered with physical punishment. The perpetrator wants this treatment because he has inflicted it on others. Some societies or governments may prohibit "cruel and unusual" punishment. But the punishment must be both cruel and unusual. If everyone who commits murder under certain circumstances gets the death penalty, then the punishment is not unusual. The perpetrator is not singled out from other murderers and punishment is consistent with the law and legal precedents.

A civil society needs to appropriately control its members who cannot control themselves.

CIVIL SOCIETY'S GOVERNMENT STRUCTURE

The middle class is best served in a participatory, elected government. In determining the best type of government, we must defer to the very wise. The founders of the United States of America could have chosen any governmental structure in the world, including a monarchy or a collective leadership council composed of an odd number of people. Instead, they created a government with checks and balances. The Senate, one half of the legislative branch, was appointed by state legislatures. (This was changed by constitutional amendment in 1913). The House of Representatives, the other half of the legislature, was popularly elected with the distribution of members based on population. The government was set up in such a way that consensus was necessary and although the majority ruled, the interests and rights of the minority were protected.

If the government is too powerful, then people who run the government are too powerful and the temptation to take personal property away from those not in power is too great. In short, "power tends to corrupt and absolute power corrupts absolutely," as English historian Lord Acton famously posited in the 19th century.

Not all societies can enjoy democracy and freedom. A country at war or under siege will relinquish democracy. Unpopular decisions, like who will be sacrificed in battle, must be made by someone not answerable to an electorate. Internal controls will be strengthened and secrecy becomes more important. Dissent becomes synonymous with aiding the enemy. People are willing to give up their freedoms and rights in exchange for security. For centuries, Russia was surrounded by enemies. It is not a surprise that their society gravitated toward an autocratic but secure system.

Not all societies should enjoy freedom and democracy. Democracy only works in a civil society. A society that has no moral compass, where lying, cheating, and stealing are permitted, and neither human life nor human existence are valued, must be controlled. Members of this kind of a society will not work for the common good.

The Italian political theorist Machiavelli wrote of this in detail circa 1513. As he expressed, an evil society deserves the evilest member as its ruler. Ascension to and usage of power is based on deceit, intimidation, force, coercion, subversion, and assassination. In Machiavelli's time, democracy had previously only existed in ancient Greece. Athens and its allies had democracy but not every member of society shared full privileges. The Greeks who lived in democratic city-states understood the importance of civil society and recorded its nature and operation in historical journals.

Machiavelli lived at a time of monarchies when governments were not representative. The middle class was very limited and corporations did not exist. Individual rights were not enforceable. Even Machiavelli expressed hope for mankind if a representative government could be established.

While a dictatorship will guarantee the marginalization of the middle class, its inverse - a representative government - will not in itself guarantee the viability of the middle class.

As Marx points out, the government is a tool of and a servant to the rich. In 2020, this is still the case. Even the most ambitious and forceful political rhetoric becomes silent once the election has passed. The rich have very effectively infiltrated democratic institutions. Even politicians who purportedly represent the common man know who ultimately controls the purse strings.

THE CURLEY EFFECT

The Curley Effect is a term coined by two professors of economics and is not meant to praise or denigrate James Michael Curley, who was a very successful politician. According to most economic models, political leaders will try to make prudent decisions and use resources wisely. In the long term, the electorate recognizes waste and corruption and will gravitate to leaders averse to that behavior. The electorate understands that individually and as a community, their wealth and well-being are maximized when their leaders are prudent. Leaders also recognize the value of maximizing the wealth and well-being of their domain. They usually get a share, in financial terms, of the equivalent of the Gross Domestic Product of the domain. The richer their community, the more tax revenue is available, and thus it becomes the more likely their government salary and side income will increase.

The prudent decision economic model does not seem to work in all cases. Many large cities and a few countries have cascaded downward economically. Despite patently corrupt leadership, the electorate of these affected locales has continued their long-term support for these rulers.

The Curley Effect describes a model where political leaders will deliberately make wasteful and corrupt decisions to further their own ends. The leader works from an "us versus them" mentality. The two sides are easily identifiable, defined in the past by ethnicity, race, gender, or immigrant status. The leader enacts programs to benefit "us." He or she might prey upon sympathy, guilt, "fairness," or other emotions to enact these programs, especially if the "us" is in the minority. He or she effectively uses the tools of deceit, intimidation, coercion, and subversion. He or she ensures government jobs and influential political appointments are given to "us."

The Curley Effect historically was implemented to somehow favor the economically disadvantaged, especially the non-contributors. As mentioned earlier in this manifesto, Marx wrote that non-contributors were actually tools of the rich. They are dependable supporters of the status quo, especially if they derive benefits without contributing to society or the economy.

The first step of the Curley Effect is to set up programs benefiting "us" while excluding "them." Once these programs are in place, the politicians begin demonizing "them." They claim that "they" don't care about "us" and if "they" ever gain power, the benefits for "us" will disappear. The real beneficiaries of the programs are the rich. Food payments from the government are ultimately delivered to grocery store owners. Housing subsidies are ultimately delivered to owners of tenements.

The attack on the middle class has started. It is a slow and grinding siege.

Step two is to increase government spending on wasteful endeavors. The government is usually the biggest customer in a domain and its maintenance programs are a steady source of income for those receiving the revenue. The leader approves certain ambitious construction projects, like a new city hall, convention center, or a bridge. The wealthy, who own construction, trash collection, utility, and other companies have contracts with the government. They eagerly join the leader to get a piece of the largesse.

The leader and his or her cronies award lucrative contracts, spending public funds much more extravagantly than any private business would spend on the same projects. The wealthy line their pockets and pay the appropriate kickbacks to government officials. James Curley openly boasted "In order to help the poor, you have to provide for yourself." Curley, who entered politics penniless, became a bank president.

Step three in the process is raising taxes. Taxes are levied and increased disproportionately on the middle class. Taxes are used to pay annual expenses and capital improvements. Since capital improvements (like a new building) involve a large initial financial outlay but can be used twenty or more years in the future, they are often financed with bonds. This matches or levels the expense of the capital improvement over its expected useful lifetime. Issuing bonds is equivalent to borrowing money.

In some governmental units (like cities), voters must approve the issuance of bonds. Historically, voters have been incredibly receptive to issuing bonds. They may be told that taxes will not increase if bonds are issued. While the statement is nominally true – the simple act of borrowing money does not create a financial burden – it is only a half-truth. Paying the interest and repaying the principal on a bond does necessitate a tax increase. When voters approve a bond issuance, they are in effect voting for a tax increase.

Authors laud the accomplishments of leaders like James Curley. They state that the successors to the office were not as productive. How could they be? The bond money had been spent, annual government expenditures had risen dramatically, and taxes had been increased to an almost unsustainable level. There was no room for more projects.

In a domain where the Curley Effect has been implemented, the middle class is damaged in two ways: Their taxes are raised and the prices they pay for food, goods, and services increase. Giving a financial subsidy to a certain segment of the population affects what economists call the "price elasticity of demand." In other words, if the price of something rises, then people buy less of it. This helps to keep prices low. When people are given subsidies, they are not as sensitive to prices and the demand for food, goods, or services increases. This keeps prices higher than they would normally be in a free market. The middle class also must pay the higher prices, reducing their disposable income. Revenue from increased prices flows to wealthy business owners as higher profit margins.

The combination of higher taxes, higher prices, demonization, lack of opportunity, and discouragement causes some members of "them" to leave the domain. "They" are members of the middle class who are not politically connected. They want employment, security, health care, some leisure, and freedom to follow their dreams.

As "they" leave the domain, the remaining electorate contains a larger proportion of the leader's supporters.

People in other domains who fit the profile of "us" begin to migrate into the domain. They either enter at random, have friends or family who are "us" already residing in the domain, or hear about the domain in the media. New migrants begin receiving the benefits of belonging to "us."

The leader has even more supporters in the electorate and eventually becomes guaranteed to win the election since his or her constituency is a comfortable majority. He or she has amassed great personal wealth from selling influence. Every year the domain becomes poorer than the year before. Every year the leader's cronies become richer. Every year the middle class becomes more hollowed out. Property values fall as fewer people want to move into the domain. Crime increases with poverty and inadequate law and code enforcement. The corruption from the top has filtered down to every public office including the police.

The Curley Effect has played out to completion. It has taken years. The changes that occurred annually were barely noticeable. The society after 50 years of waste and corruption is completely alien to the society it spawned from. The leader has increased his or her political base through distortionary, wealth-reducing policies. It is easy to destroy a society, hard to build one.

What remains after 50 years is a domain requiring financial support from a larger domain or neighboring domains. Of course, most of the support is siphoned off by the rich while the electorate exists in a community without employment, security, health care, or the hope of something better.

The domain is ruled by the evilest member of society. Machiavelli is proven right after all.

The prudent decision economic model and the Curley Effect economic model differ mathematically. The prudent decision model is based on a static population. No one moves in or out of the domain. The Curley Effect model allows for changes in the population. It also allows people in the population to be treated differently.

JUST US

Society needs to preclude or counteract the implementation of bad decisions, wasteful spending, and creating an "us versus them" environment. Let's call the new guiding principles "Just Us."

The most important mechanism to ensure Just Us would be a fundamental law or constitutional provision stating that if one citizen is entitled to some government benefit simply by being alive, then all citizens are entitled to the same benefit.

A civil society with adequate resources will not allow its weakest members to be neglected. A civil society will at least feed, clothe, shelter, and provide some medical services to them. However, these services do not necessarily need to be provided by the government.

The type or level of care needed for a child differs from that of an adult. The weakest child would be an orphan. An orphan needs parental care, nurturing, education, and the level of safety and protection that all children should have.

If the government enacted a program to benefit the poor, then the program would have to benefit the middle class and the rich on equal terms. This does not mean devising a complicated formula or sliding scale that depends on income. It means if one adult receives 10 units a month to buy food, then every adult receives 10 units a month to buy food. If a family of four receives 200 units per month for housing, then every family of four gets 200 units per month for housing. There is no means testing and the units can be used to pay rent, pay a mortgage, or applied to any other purpose in case a home is owned outright.

Medical care is not a right. It is a transaction between a doctor and a patient, not between a doctor and the government. A civil society may choose to provide a certain level of medical care for all citizens, administered by a government-run health care system and implemented through a network of public clinics.

Tax revenues would pay for the clinics and every citizen would be welcome. Young and old alike could receive care and clinics may even be open 24 hours a day. A citizen may opt to seek care from private physicians, paying the cost personally, or securing health insurance to cover unexpected large expenses. Some medical care may simply not be available in public clinics or even from the private sector. Much depends on the resources of society.

Many necessities, like food and clothing, can and probably should be provided through the church. In 2020, many organizations provide food to indigents even though government programs do the same. If there were no government food programs, churches and other charities would clamber over each other to fill the void. Distributing necessities enhances relationships within a community. People seeking free food travel the shortest distance possible. People also attend church or volunteer close to their home, giving them a chance to meet others.

The church may have avenues for those wishing to volunteer. Through volunteering, members of a community have more chances to meet their neighbors. Sometimes, while serving, a diligent volunteer meets another individual who offers employment to the volunteer. Community service also obviates an entitlement mentality and the smug, self-centered countenance.

A civil society is a fair society. It is only fair that if one citizen has a right to something, then all citizens have an equal right to the same. The Just Us model mathematically changes the Curley Effect model by removing the ability to reward one segment of society and punish another.

Government subsidies or payments for living expenses did not exist at the time of Marx. It would be interesting to hear the opinion of communists of Marx's time on the welfare state 200 years later.

CONTROLLING PUBLIC CORRUPTION

Another integral part of "Just Us" is a fundamental right to good government. Most of the developed world operates under some form of representative government. The founders of the United States of America understood and appreciated the necessity of checks and balances within a representative government.

The section of this manifesto titled The Middle Class and the Nature and Size of Government addressed controlling the size of government. In the next century, the various societies in the world must extend the checks and balances ideology to government (leaders, politicians, and bureaucrats) behavior. No longer will it be acceptable to hide behind the "people voted for this" excuse.

Other tools are available to thwart the corrupt leader who impoverishes his or her domain.

If the domain is a city or some other part of a nation, then the national government could impose restraints. In many instances, cities receive funds or grants for various initiatives from the national government. As part of Just Us, the national government could impose guidelines, like a ratio of spending per capita to the average income of the lower 90% of the domain's members. This gives leaders an incentive to improve the fortunes of the middle class. If spending rose above the guidelines, then the national government could impose a variety of consequences on the domain. These include but are not limited to reducing financial assistance, imposing outside management with accountability to the national government or even a religious organization, or levying an excise tax on every individual or business with an income above a certain threshold.

The national government could enact a law making it more difficult for a poorly managed or corrupt domain to issue bonds. The law would protect middle-class investors from financial loss from these bonds. The law would require that, in the event of a default, the brokerage house or sponsor of the issuance would be liable to its customers. The law would also hold investment firms that manage mutual funds and retirement accounts responsible to their clientele for losses from government bonds. It would apply to funds in which more than 15% of the participants have an average income in the lower 90% of citizens nationally.

Bond default protection would not extend to private placements with extremely wealthy people. In all other cases, the brokerage houses and mutual fund managers would be forced to do due diligence. They could not protect their wealthy individuals by passing deteriorating credit risk from wealthy clients to middle-class clients.

With forced public accountability, it would be more difficult for an unscrupulous leader to enrich himself or herself while simultaneously impoverishing his or her domain. James Curley, for example, continued to be elected despite the electorate's knowledge of his corruption. He went to jail during one of his mayoral terms but was released early and given a presidential pardon.

This story illustrates two important points. First, it is a sad statement on the character of the electorate. They chose food over principles, corruption over virtue, and temporary comfort over long term prosperity. Their view of what was in their greatest self-interest shows a fundamental lack of understanding at best and an incorrigible Machiavellian mentality at worst. Such citizens will not form or be members of a civil society. Second, it reveals the pervasiveness of corruption and control of the wealthy. The wealthy influence national, regional, and city governments and, by extension, control all significant financial arrangements. "Equal protection under the law" somehow exempts the rich and powerful. Abuse of power will occur and continue as long as the electorate does not understand the importance of restraints on those in power and does not demand that a civil society impose such restraints.

GOOD GOVERNANCE EXAMPLES

Fortunately, there are examples of good governance we can refer to and learn from. One example was the Homestead Act of 1862 in the United States of America. Several similar laws enacted before and after the Homestead Act had the same purpose and effect. The Homestead Act opened public land to private ownership. A person could get ownership of a limited area of land (160 acres) if he or she built a house on the land and farmed the acreage for a minimum of five years.

In the 19th century, farming was difficult work. The use of hand implements was required to clear timber and brush. Horses pulled plows but planting and harvesting required intensive human labor. Access to water was essential and not every parcel of land was arable. The people availing themselves of the opportunity the Homestead Act offered were hard-working and self-sufficient.

The Homestead Act bolstered the middle class in many ways.

First, the amount of land eligible to be given to any individual was limited. Each individual was allowed only one tract of land. No one received a huge estate. Tract size was determined so that each tract could support a viable farm with income-producing crops. The goal of ownership was not merely subsistence farming.

Second, both the government and farmers acted ethically. Government representatives set up tracts fairly and recorded the deeds correctly once conditions of ownership were satisfied. Farmers adhered to the rules of ownership. They were fundamentally honest, a trait developed through their religious beliefs. Because of the hard manual labor involved, no one had time to think about gaming the system or cheating a neighbor. Farmers could rely on the word of the government, knowing that once the rules of ownership were met, they permanently and legally owned their farm, with no chance that it could somehow be confiscated.

Third, the program attracted people with a certain work ethic - the most diligent of the citizenry. Most came from a farming background so they understood that sometimes they would work from dawn to dusk. They also traded fairly and paid a reasonable wage for a day's work. They expected a fair price for their produce as well.

Fourth, the Homestead Act fostered a sense of community. In farming communities, the difference between the richest and the poorest was rather modest. Store owners and bankers were at one end and laborers at the other, but the concentration of assets and income was squarely on the middle class. Members of a community had to rely on each other. The Homestead Act required the signatures of two unrelated witnesses attesting that the acreage was occupied and cultivated before a settler could secure ownership of his or her land. During the peaks of planting and harvesting seasons, the entire community came together and assisted each other. Barn building was also a community event. Neighbors helped each other for free, and no one kept records on who may have helped most.

Fifth, everyone was welcome. No special subprograms or conditions favored or discouraged any identifiable subgroup of the citizenry. All participants had two things in common – the desire to earn a farm and a strong moral character. The communities created were diverse in terms of ethnic backgrounds and religious beliefs.

Was the administration of the law perfect? Absolutely not. Land speculators and squatters snatched up the most desirable tracts. Many squatters who should have been forcibly removed from the land were allowed to stay. There were instances of forgery. But the law enabled over a million citizens to establish residence on former public land.

Another example of good governance is found in the state of Utah in the United States of America. The region was first settled in the 1840s by members of The Church of Jesus Christ of Latter-day Saints, otherwise known as the Mormons. In the 1890s, Utah became a state. From statehood until 2020, the Church of Latter-day Saints has greatly influenced Utah. The percentage of residents identifying themselves as Latter-day Saints was near 100% in the 1890s and is now two-thirds in 2020. Utah has seen substantial immigration by members of other denominations since statehood.

The Church of Jesus Christ is very demanding. Young men are required to perform a two-year mission after finishing high school. Church attendance is mandatory, as are monthly group meetings, community service, tithing, fasting, and abstinence from certain substances. Members of the Church of Jesus Christ are almost universally good and honest people. If you are fortunate enough to work for one, you know you will be treated fairly – not because the law mandates it but because his or her religion instills underlying values of decency and honesty.

The Latter-day Saints are family oriented. They are persistent in bringing others into the faith. They do not force their faith on others or use it as a weapon against others. Even though the Church of Jesus Christ is demanding, it has been quite successful at converting others. The states surrounding Utah have seen an increase in the number of Church of Jesus Christ members within their borders.

The Church of Jesus Christ of Latter-day Saints exerts influence over Utah's state and local governments. The Church maintains a Public Affairs Committee that meets with elected officials from all political parties. The Public Affairs Committee, comprised of theological experts, advises on whether proposed legislation is consistent with church scripture and doctrine. The elected officials are legal or secular experts. The two work together to craft the best possible laws and regulations. The committee is mindful of other faiths and is surprisingly tolerant. They do not exercise as much power as they could.

The State of Utah is not a theocracy, a government ruled by religious leaders. The Church of Latter-day Saints provides guidance and discipline. It prevents opportunism exhibited by politicians who might be drawn to the Curley effect.

Has the governmental structure of Utah been successful for the middle class? As measured by the United States Department of Commerce, in 2020, Utah ranked 14th highest out of 50 states for median household income. This is impressive considering Utah has no seacoast and cannot import or export easily. Even more striking, Utah has the least income inequality of all the states. The rich are not exceedingly rich and the poor are not destitute. Statistically, the welfare of the middle class is highest in Utah.

For a third example of good governance, we turn to the Stroganov family in Russia. The first historical reference to the Stroganovs appears around 1400, and the economic dynasty ended during the Russian Revolution of 1917. For over 500 years they were economic leaders and held a great deal of influence in a society where political power was concentrated in a king (or "tsar" in the Russian language). The tsar could, on a whim, imprison any subject of the realm and transfer that subject's possessions to someone else.

The Stroganovs owned or managed several businesses. In the 1400s, they used the money earned from trading to buy land in the far north of Russia. They also managed land for nobility and first became recognized by nobility when a Stroganov paid a ransom for a kidnapped prince.

The Stroganov family bought land around Solvychegodsk, a town of 2,000 inhabitants, and moved there in 1500. The town sat at the base of mountains rich in salt, gold, iron ore, semiprecious stones, and timber. The first industries to develop were the easiest. In 1520, two Stroganov brothers opened a salt mine, a salt refinery, and a lumber facility. It was hard physical labor under harsh conditions. At the time, there was tremendous profit in salt. From the outset, the Stroganovs paid their workers well.

The most influential member of the family was Anika Stroganov (Russian spelling and pronunciation may vary). In the 1550s, he traveled to Moscow where he convinced the tsar to grant him land for mining and logging. In the 1560s, Stroganov was given control over an expanded area covering the Ural Mountains. His total land holdings reached 8.5 million acres or 34,000 square kilometers.

The Stroganovs took their responsibilities very seriously. In addition to salt mining and logging, they built towns, which required many construction workers. They established iron ore mining and iron smelters. They expanded farming. They maintained a private army to defend against the eastern marauders. They built fortresses for defense, some of which also served as residences.

The Stroganovs created thousands of middle-class jobs. In the 1500s, Russia was firmly locked into the feudal system of economics and government. Serfs were the equivalent of slaves. They could not own land. They could not leave the estate and, if the estate was sold, the serfs were sold with it. Serfdom was unlike other types of slavery where slaves were bought and sold as separate property. Serfdom in Russia was abolished in 1861 at about the same time slavery was abolished in the United States.

The northern and Ural mountain provinces in Russia had very little serfdom. These were the areas under Stroganov control or ownership. The Stroganovs instead concentrated on industry, which required more skilled labor and paid more than adequate wages. The other provinces seemed content to remain in a feudal system.

How did the Stroganov family manage their conglomerate of industries spread over an immense land area? First, each operating unit had a manager. The manager was required to meet a production quota. The quota was quite demanding but achievable through hard work. The Stroganovs, having worked in their industries, knew first-hand what was achievable and what was impossible. Travel at that time was difficult. The fastest way was by watercraft. Rivers froze over during the long, cold Russian winters. Those who traveled by land rode horseback or in horse-drawn vehicles. Even under these conditions, the Stroganovs made it a point to visit every operation as many times as possible. They evaluated production not only for themselves but to verify what tax collectors reported. The tsar also sent representatives throughout the kingdom to verify all agricultural and industrial production.

Another unique approach the Stroganovs took was in the relatively low amount of wealth they retained for themselves. As owners, they decided how much to keep after paying taxes. Workers far and wide sought employment from the Stroganovs. Managers were demanding, but pay for performance was excellent.

The Stroganovs kept a few large residences adorned with beautiful decorations that housed many valuables, as did other members of Russian nobility. Around 1700, the tsar formally elevated the Stroganov patriarch to the noble status of baron. Many family members subsequently married into nobility.

The Stroganovs did not hoard their money or spend it solely on themselves. They donated large sums to the Russian government in addition to paying taxes. A large percentage of the donations were used for national defense.

The Stroganovs were devout Russian Orthodox Christians. Like the Catholic Church in Western Europe, the various Eastern Orthodox Churches in Eastern Europe were closely aligned with their respective nations, receiving financial support from each country. The Stroganovs used personal wealth to build churches throughout their domain. Some churches were large and became famous, while others were smaller in scale and notability.

They were also patrons of the arts, funding the Saint Petersburg Academy of Art and founding the Stroganov Institute of Applied Arts in Moscow. In the 1800s, the Stroganovs endowed many hospitals, schools, churches, and monasteries. Their religion propelled them to do right and benefit others. Anika Stroganov became a monk in the 1560s during his final years of life, as his father had done. The church was grateful for his financial as well as personal support.

The Stroganov family presided over a long period of economic vitality because it created an environment friendly to the middle class. They thought of and treated their middle-class employees as fellow men. The wage structure within their businesses was much flatter than similar businesses at the time. Their employees responded with high productivity and high revenues. Plenty of wealth was shared with the tsars. The Stroganovs were grounded in their Christian faith, which stressed the value of human beings. Their success is measured by their tenure – 500 years. They kept the tsars happy and retained their positions of leadership during uncertain times.

History has examples where the middle class flourished or at least improved its status. Identifying environments that either fostered or decimated the middle class is important. We can analyze situations throughout history to discover fundamental beneficial principles. We can apply the same principles to new environments and circumstances. We can also learn from failures and try to avoid those situations.

As noted previously, destroying a society is much easier than building one. Likewise, destroying the middle class is much easier than constructing it. In our limited examples, we see the willingness of the middle class to exist and grow. Most people will never be rich but most have aspirations to improve their lives.

THE PARETO DISTRIBUTION

Empirical evidence reveals that the distribution of wealth (assets or income) within a society follows a Pareto distribution, which is a statistical function or formula. Much has been written on this subject in a myriad of sources so this manifesto will mention only a few of the most relevant points.

The distribution of wealth in society may follow a Pareto curve no matter the economic environment. There will always be destitute people and people with unimaginable wealth. The middle class might be defined as the interval on the Pareto curve above the bottom 15% and below the top 15%.

Mathematically, the Pareto function has a scaling component and a shape component. The shape component is called "alpha" - the larger alpha is, the more wealth is concentrated among the wealthiest individuals in society.

The larger the community, the larger the alpha. This is both intuitive and observed in the real world. A village of 20 households probably will not have extreme differences in wealth. Statistically, starting with 100 people and adding one person at a time to the sample, eventually the most recent person added will be richer or poorer than everyone else.

Due to the scaling component, the richer the community, the larger the spread between the richest and poorest. If one community is twice as rich as its neighbor, then the gap between richest and poorest will also be twice as much. The alpha is unchanged.

From 1900 to 1910, Vilfredo Pareto discovered and published the economic phenomenon bearing his name. After earning a doctorate in engineering, Pareto applied his interest in equilibrium analysis to the disciplines of economics and sociology. He based his paper on years of research, scouring financial records of any and every kind. He examined records from the 1450s to the 1890s, studying data from Germany, France, Switzerland, Britain, Prussia, and Peru. He looked at data from large and small populations. All data supported a common statistical function – a Pareto function with scaling and shape components. Pareto found that the alpha could vary but in all cases, a small number of rich people owned or controlled most of the wealth.

Subsequent research on several countries' income tax records up to the present day supports Pareto's conclusions. Again, distinguishing assets from income is imperative. Recent studies used income tax returns to determine the alpha for societies under consideration. The real alphas are much higher than analyses indicate because poor individuals derive all their income from wages. For rich individuals, some if not most of their income comes from assets, including businesses. An example is shown below:

Table 56: Example of the Income Ratio and Asset Ratio used to Assess Alpha

	Poor Person		Rich Person
(1) Assets	1,000 units		100,000 units
(2) Income from Assets	100 units		10,000 units
(3) Income from Labor	9,900 units		20,000 units
(4) Total Income	10,000 units		30,000 units
(5) Income Ratio (Rich line 4/Poor line 4)		3.0	
(6) Asset Ratio (Rich line 1/Poor line 1)		100.0	

From the perspective of Income, it appears that the rich person is three times wealthier than the poor person, but this measurement is understated. The real ratio is 100.

Pareto's work came 50 to 60 years after Marx's *Communist Manifesto*. Marx did not have this information when he wrote the manifesto and might have reached different conclusions had this data been available.

Very familiar with *The Communist Manifesto*, Pareto wrote that Socialism was inconsistent with reality. A sustainable socialist society had never been seen throughout the entire history of man because it was mathematically, economically, and socially impossible. Orderly, peaceful societies have always had an economic order as well, with relatively few wealthy members and a preponderance of poor members.

Pareto also had two other important insights: First, he wrote and lectured about the importance of ethics and recommended that religion be taught as a fundamental part of any school's curriculum. Second, he believed that an elected government was ineffective in bringing about a more supportive system for the middle class because the elite and aristocrats gain control of the elected officials. They then use the institution of an elected government to further their own economic and other interests.

This manifesto started with a reference to ancient Egypt. The common perception of ancient Egypt is that of millions of slaves spending their lives enhancing the life of and building a tomb for the leader. The reality was very different.

Ancient Egypt lasted as a culture for 3,000 years. They must have done something worth replicating.

Throughout ancient Egypt's existence, enemies occupied parts of the realm, which later were brought back under Egyptian control, then retaken by enemies. Different families ascended to the position of pharaoh. Inventions changed life over time – notably the use of copper, then the production and use of iron. Trade with neighboring regions brought wealth and new products into Egypt. Egypt was the world's producer of papyrus paper. Many small businesses were engaged in weaving cloth and making clothes from flax. Their civilization was actually quite dynamic.

The Egyptians shared a common ethical belief system called Ma'at. The pharaoh was the lord of Ma'at and ultimately responsible for making good laws and keeping the gods happy. Ma'at represented truth, balance, order, harmony, law, morality, and justice. The pharaoh was expected to follow Ma'at and to put the health and happiness of his subjects first. Everyone also believed that the gods created each of them and placed each in his or her role in the world. As a consequence, each person was to be happy with his or her lot in life.

In ancient Egypt, resources were spent building pyramids containing considerable - but not necessarily enormous - wealth. Pyramids were not considered private property. Present-day counterparts, at least in terms of how the government spends its resources, would be public facilities and assets like parks, natural preserves and wetlands, government buildings, museums, public transportation, space exploration, dams and nuclear power plants, and public infrastructure.

Towns and cities were organized into neighborhoods according to house size. Generally, the child learned the trade of the parent so there was little opportunity to rise above the class from which one was born. The ratio of the largest to the smallest house was perhaps 10 to 1. There were many farms - most of modest size. Slaves comprised only about 1% of the population, unusually tiny for societies in the ancient world. Pyramids were built by laborers who were free men.

Ancient Egypt's distribution of wealth was flatter than in the countries of today. In terms of the Pareto distribution, their alpha was much lower. This might be counterintuitive but is supported by the following two considerations:

First, less wealth and fewer people existed 2,000 years ago. Ancient Egypt's population rose from about one million in 3000 BC to five million in 1 AD.

Second, look at the cities of today. Someone owns every skyscraper. Someone owns every factory, every retail store, and every house. Objects of art and jewels not placed in the public domain are also owned by someone. Since the time of ancient Egypt, 2,000 years of art has been created. There are people today with immense wealth – wealth that most of the population cannot even fathom.

To summarize the discussion of the Pareto distribution, economic and social institutions follow a mathematical and statistical function. The model has withstood much scrutiny. Past closeness-of-fit measurements and model scenario testing reveal that programs that lower the alpha raise the well-being of the middle class. Programs benefiting the middle class also benefit the poor. The results from mathematical iterations over a long time horizon show total GDP growth is larger if the alpha is smaller. In other words, a society with programs benefiting the middle class becomes the richest society for everyone.

COMMUNISM AND THE FAMILY

What is the end game? Many people who claim to follow Marx's ideology do not understand this simple question. Assuming a society has adopted the tenets of communism or socialism and no further change is required, what does that society look like? Will people be happier than they are today?

The Communist Manifesto is intellectually honest and internally consistent. Marx tells the reader the character of and relationships within a society governed by communism. The flag bearers for communism or socialism are the flag bearers for the future it creates, the behavior it creates, and the prosperity it creates.

Marx is very clear that communism is not compatible with the family as we know it. He describes the society under communism as hedonistic, especially regarding sensual matters. Marriage is not a desirable arrangement and should be scuttled as no longer relevant. People who would follow a committed relationship are to be ridiculed. In Marx's society, every person should enjoy the company of as many other people as possible. Families tend to interfere with the pursuit of pleasure. Marx never did reveal how children of the communist society should be raised.

He supports his view of the future by noting the stress that families of the 1840s experienced. At the time, both parents of urban labor class families usually had to work. Children went to work as early as age nine (allowed by law). Children not working often roamed the streets unsupervised. Wages and working conditions for children were especially deplorable. Observing conditions during the first half of the 19th century, Marx concluded that families didn't exist for urban laborers. It would be fairer to make the family life of professionals, the elite and agricultural workers consistent with that of urban workers.

History has shown that various developed societies dealt with child labor but thankfully not as Marx would have.

Marx's accounts of the role of family and promiscuity are clearly written in *The Communist Manifesto*. It is easy to verify – simply read it... unless of course, your copy was from the Soviet Union. In the Soviet Union, the Communist Party made *The Communist Manifesto* required reading for all citizens. However, their version was redacted and many communists who thought they were experts on Marx and Engels are surprised to learn otherwise.

Marx's vision of communal life and the dissolution of the family has two problems. First, families seem to be the natural way that mankind has lived for the last 5,000 years. All archeological evidence shows family structures of some sort. Ancient Egyptian records show census information by family. The genealogical records kept in India for thousands of years show families. The historical records of China and Japan reference families. 80% of Rome's population was comprised of families even though the elite were notoriously licentious and 15 to 20% of the population were slaves.

Second, children do not raise themselves. Scientific evidence gathered between the 1930s and 1950s show the effects of neglect during the early ages of childhood. Most viewers become anguished when watching films of infants rocking themselves or trying to find intellectual stimulation by using repetitive hand motions. There is no substitute for a mother's love. Infancy is the time in life when personal and constant interaction is vital for normal development.

Sadly, the effects of childhood neglect on adults have been abundantly documented. Suffice it to say that a society in which children are raised communally so that adults can pursue hedonism can be expected to have problems. This is the society where communism is the ideal form of government.

THE MIDDLE CLASS AND WORLD DEMOGRAPHICS

Demographics are the statistical characteristics of a population. Certain characteristics are identified as important, and the population is sorted and studied by those characteristics. The population is also projected into the future, using assumptions for the magnitude of key drivers, like birth rate, net immigration, and death rate.

In theory, the population of a new organism (including man) in a confined environment rises exponentially over time when initially introduced to that environment. As the population grows, its rate of growth slows to a more linear increase. When the population reaches the natural carrying capacity of its environment, the rate of growth becomes zero. The population becomes static at that point, and the number of births is equal to the number of deaths.

A logistic growth rate is one that slows as a population nears the natural carrying capacity. If a population somehow exceeds the environment's natural carrying capacity, then Mother Nature takes whatever steps necessary to bring it under control.

How close are humans to reaching Earth's natural carrying capacity? The answer is complicated. From a purely biological standpoint, it could happen as early as 2100. If humans adopted a more vegetarian diet, land use would shift to greater efficiency, allowing for more people to exist.

A food crisis can occur in a population that has not reached the environment's natural carrying capacity. Societal and behavioral dynamics can strain the use of resources. First, the geographical distribution of the population differs greatly from the geographical locations of food production. Massive sprawling cities are found on every continent save Antarctica. Within these cities, large-scale food production is absent. To meet an urban population's food consumption, tons and tons of food must be brought in daily. Feeding an urban population requires reliable transportation, reliable energy sources powering transportation, a reliable food supply, accessible food distribution centers, and an ethical, orderly population. If any of these requirements are somehow not met, a local crisis could potentially occur.

The second dynamic is hoarding. A small, localized supply interruption will cause many people to hoard. An example of localized hoarding occurs when tropical storms affect an area of America's Gulf Coast where many of the nation's oil refineries are located. Should a hurricane threaten Houston, people in other Texas cities will fuel up their autos and fill gas containers since they know refinery production could be interrupted for a few days. This hoarding causes temporary supply shortages.

People hoard because they have a self-preservation mentality. They will ensure that they have an abundance, even if it means their neighbor goes without. A crisis may bring out the best in people but often shows them at their worst. During World War II, most governments imposed a rationing system by issuing cards to citizens. These cards allowed the holder to purchase a limited quantity of a certain food item. The stated purpose of rationing was to ensure enough food for the soldiers. Their true purpose was to prevent hoarding. People will hoard food only to discard it later if hoarding assures their survival.

The geographical distribution of the population and the phenomenon of hoarding increase the likelihood of food shortages, whether local, regional or worldwide. Ever-increasing urban populations make food shortages more likely.

What are the unique impacts of overpopulation on the middle class?

In the event of a food shortage, the entire economy shifts. Banking and insurance jobs are incidental at best to the procurement of food and therefore unnecessary. Restaurants would close. Even industries considered vital, like medical care, oil and gas, and transportation would have employee absenteeism and disruption. Some jobs would vanish while other labor needs would emerge. Most likely, aggregate wages and GDP would plummet.

If a food shortage occurs, the political structure changes. Any government in place at the onset of the crisis would be deemed ineffective. A new set of leaders would assume power. Often a nation's military takes control, but this is not an inevitability. Generally, the largest and most organized group within a nation will step into the leadership roles. The new leaders might need to make unpleasant but necessary changes to the nation to prevent future food shortages and remain in power.

The world in 2020 is already experiencing overpopulation and its effects.

The fertility rate is the most important demographic characteristic in a population. It tells how many children per woman there are in a country or other political subdivision. It is useful as a predictor of the future population and therefore the future demand for resources. A value of slightly above 2.0 is consistent with a stable population (one each for the father and mother, plus an allowance for child mortality).

The table below shows projected populations for various fertility rates. In each case, the starting population is 1,000. Other models may produce slightly different results.

Table 57: Projected Populations for Various Fertility Rates and Beginning Population of 1,000

Fertility Rate Number of children per woman	Estimated Population in 20 Years	Estimated Population in 50 Years
1.5	820	600
1.75	890	750
2.0	1,000	1,000
2.25	1,050	1,120
2.5	1,130	1,360
2.75	1,220	1,640
3.0	1,310	1,960
3.5	1,500	2,770
4.0	1,720	3,860
4.5	1,950	5,300
5.0	2,200	7,210
5.5	2,480	9,730
6.0	2,800	13,010

A society or segment of a society with a high fertility rate of 5.0 children per woman will double its population in 20 years. In 60 years, the population will increase ten times. There are countries or regions in 2020 with fertility rates of this magnitude. This creates a myriad of economic and social problems.

In 2020, many countries are net food importers. There are several reasons for this. Some countries have high labor costs, making food production uncompetitive with other countries. Some have inadequate infrastructure. Some have onerous regulations, making food production impossible. Most net food importers have too many people and not enough land.

This manifesto will not single out any particular country. It should be noted that the presentation of facts often depends on how the underlying data is combined. For instance, Country A is a net importer of 1,000 units of food. Country B is a net exporter of 1,100 units of food. If these are aggregated into a single region, one would conclude that the region was a food exporter of 100 units. This masks a potential problem, especially if Country A's fertility rate is 4.0 and Country B's fertility rate is 1.5. This manifesto will identify instances of dissimilar aggregation.

In 2020, countries or regions that are net food importers in most cases import a modest portion of food needed for their populations. South America feeds the rest of the world and can supply the modest import needs of other nations. Analogous to the situation of transporting food from rural to urban areas within a country, the global mismatch between where food is produced and where it is consumed carries certain risks.

Certain regions of the world will be examined. This is a snapshot in time, based on conditions in 2020. Future conditions and relationships will change, but there is great value in identifying or estimating current resource needs, current mismatches, future populations, future resource needs, and future mismatches. Any methodology used to estimate the future must make assumptions regarding conditions and relationships in the future. Any research will start with a baseline, where assumed future conditions and relationships are similar to the current ones. The impact of expected changes in behavior can be quantified, and over time actual results can be compared to past expectations, and variances can be explained. Most research will not deliberately paint either a rosy picture or a dark landscape but will identify the conditions leading to those scenarios.

This manifesto will limit itself to working with future estimates which are close to the current situation. These will be the baseline assumptions. An entire book could be written on future demographics under various initiatives.

In this manifesto, East Asia includes Indochina and the Pacific Region, Japan, and China. In this diverse region, most countries are food exporters except China and Japan, which are large importers. In the table below, the Percentage of Food Imported is net imports, which is imports less exports, divided by total food consumed. A country or region exporting food will have a negative value. The Percentage of Food Imported in 20 Years is an estimate that assumes food production will remain at current levels. Food consumption is dependent on population, so an increasing population will import more food and a decreasing population will import less. A country that exports food but has an increasing population may become a net importer and vice versa.

In the table below, the last line - Total East Asia - is the sum or aggregation of the prior three lines. China and Japan are identified separately because they are dissimilar to the rest of the countries in the region.

Table 58: Demographics and Food Requirements for East Asia

Region	Current Population (millions)	Fertility Rate	Percentage of Food Imported	Percentage of Food Imported in 20 Years
East Asia w/o Japan or China	805	2.1	(1.6 %)	0.7%
China	1,420	1.6	3.6%	(16.0%)
Japan	127	1.5	16.0%	(3.0%)
Total East Asia	2,352	1.8	4.1%	(6.3%)

The table above shows that in East Asia, low fertility rates will alleviate the need to import significant amounts of food. The two major importers could become exporters while the other nations in the region could become marginal importers as a group.

North Africa and the Middle East extends from Morocco in the west to Pakistan in the east. These countries have similar cultures and religions.

In 2020, this region has a relatively high fertility rate of 2.9 children per woman. Furthermore, this arid region cannot agriculturally sustain its current population.

Table 59: Demographics and Food Requirements for North Africa and the Middle East				
Region	Current Population (millions)	Fertility Rate	Percentage of Food Imported	Percentage of Food Imported in 20 Years
North Africa and the Middle East	869	2.9	9.9 %	29.2%

This region should give the rest of the world concern. The pressure to emigrate from the region already exists. In the next 20 years, this pressure will only intensify. The lack of resources creates instability and most people crave stability. The high fertility rate in an already crowded region means there simply is no place left to live. Plenty of desert land exists but the absence of water means the absence of people. Without people, there are no economic opportunities and no reason to settle the area. If fresh water could be brought cheaply and reliably to some arid regions, urban communities could be established around other activities such as mining.

Europe seems to be the destination of choice for emigrating Middle Easterners. Europe's statistics are shown below:

Table 60: Demographics and Food Requirements for Europe				
Region	Current Population (millions)	Fertility Rate	Percentage of Food Imported	Percentage of Food Imported in 20 Years
Europe	530	1.6	1.6 %	(16.1%)

Like East Asia, Europe has a very low fertility rate. Although they currently import a small fraction of food, the expected decrease in population means Europe will have excess food in the future. However, if migration from Africa and Asia into Europe continues, the estimated number of people in Europe would be much higher than the projection using a model based on fertility rate alone. Due to net immigration, Europe might continue to import food to feed the immigrant population. Also, Europe is a relatively crowded continent with little unused arable land.

South America, which feeds the world in 2020, will be a food exporter for a long time.

Table 61: Demographics and Food Requirements for South America				
Region	Current Population (millions)	Fertility Rate	Percentage of Food Imported	Percentage of Food Imported in 20 Years
South America	656	2.1	(19.4 %)	(18.2%)

In this manifesto, South America includes the continent of South America, Central America, and Mexico. South America and Central America have similar economies. Mexico is a net food exporter with a more modest Percentage of Food Imported than other countries. All the countries in the South American group have similar fertility rates.

South American countries have a reasonable fertility rate and are expected to remain significant food exporters in the future. It should be noted that Australia and New Zealand also export a substantial amount of food.

Sub-Saharan Africa presents a grave threat to the stability of the planet and the well-being of the middle class in all countries. They have a very high fertility rate. The region's population is expected to double in 20 years. Currently, Sub-Saharan Africa feeds itself. A doubling of the population will necessitate expanding agriculture. Otherwise, Sub-Saharan Africa will need to import half of its food. Conceptually, 788 million people live in this region. They produce enough food to feed 788 million people. If the population doubles, then they must feed 788 million more. If internal food production cannot be increased, that food must be imported.

Table 62: Demographics and Food Requirements for Sub-Saharan Africa				
Region	Current Population (millions)	Fertility Rate	Percentage of Food Imported	Percentage of Food Imported in 20 Years
Sub-Saharan Africa	788	4.9	(0.3 %)	53.4%

It is often stated that the economy of Sub-Saharan Africa is primarily agricultural, comprised of subsistence farming. The families who work the farms need a large number of children, much like other parts of the world did in the 1800s. This comparison and conclusion are not supported by facts.

There are three fallacies in this reasoning:

First, the child mortality in the 1800s was orders of magnitude higher than in 2020 Africa. Penicillin had not been developed in the 1800s. Vaccines were in their infancy, difficult to obtain, and available for only a few dreaded diseases. Child (ages 5 and under) mortality worldwide in the 1800s exceeded 40%. In most of Europe, the United States, and Canada one in three children died before age 5. Adult mortality, including mothers giving birth, was also high. In this kind of environment, families needed as many children as possible.

Child mortality worldwide in 2020 is under 4%. It has fallen in most of Sub-Saharan Africa to somewhere between 5 and 6%. It is half the rate of 1990. Areas with the highest child mortality (over 10%) are embroiled in wars. In this kind of environment, children are almost assured of living into adulthood and families should consider limiting the number of children.

Second, the availability of labor in the 1800s was significantly lower than in 2020 Africa. In the United States of America, the population density of a typical rural state was 12 people per square kilometer. Many states were very sparsely inhabited, having less than 1 person per square kilometer. By contrast, the population density in a typical African nation is 220 people per square kilometer, with sparsely populated areas having 38 people per square kilometer. In Sub-Saharan Africa, labor is readily available. Reliance on family members living under one roof is not necessary.

Third, transportation and communication are very different. The slowest truck can usually go faster than the fastest horse. Farm laborers can be brought in quickly and easily. Notice of help wanted can be communicated immediately and widely.

Another thought to consider: According to several sources, about 70% of a typical Sub-Saharan country's population is engaged in agriculture. This means that 30% of the population does not need a large family and huge differences in urban versus rural family sizes should be evident.

The world community needs to understand why families are so large in Sub-Saharan Africa and how the situation can be changed.

Some regions on the planet are expected to demand more food while other regions will demand less. What does the overall picture look like? The tables below provide information for the entire world.

Table 63: Demographics, Food Production, and Food Consumption by Region in 2020 (based on 2016 to 2018)

Region	Current Population	Fertility Rate	Food Produced	Food Consumed	Percentage Imported
East Asia	2,352	1.8	2,011	2,098	4.1%
India	1,568	2.3	530	526	(0.8%)
N Africa and Mid East	869	2.9	695	771	9.9%
Sub-Sahara Africa	788	4.9	672	670	(0.3%)
S America	656	2.1	850	712	(19.4%)
Europe	530	1.6	1,127	1,145	1.6%
US & Canada	366	1.9	882	873	(1.0%)
Russia	201	1.8	230	224	(2.7%)
Australia	30	1.8	111	89	(24.7%)
Total	7,360		7,108	7,108	0.0%

In the table above, the lines labeled India, Russia, and Australia include a few neighboring countries. The Current Population is in millions. Food Produced and Food Consumed are in a common currency unit. Food includes grains and vegetables, meat and animal products, and processed food. The Food Produced or Food Consumed per person varies by region because the mix of food varies by region. The higher the proportion of grains and vegetables, the lower the per person rate.

Table 64: Projected Demographics, Food Production, and Food Consumption by Region in 2040 – Very Likely Future Situation					
Region	Current Population	Fertility Rate	Food Produced	Food Consumed	Percentage Imported
East Asia	2,122	1.8	2,011	1,892	(6.3%)
India	1,669	2.3	530	560	5.4%
N Africa and Mid East	1,105	2.9	695	982	29.2%
Sub-Sahara Africa	1,696	4.9	672	1,441	53.4%
S America	662	2.1	850	719	(18.2%)
Europe	449	1.6	1,127	971	(16.1%)
US & Canada	351	1.9	882	836	(5.5%)
Russia	188	1.8	230	209	(10.0%)
Australia	27	1.8	111	81	(37.0%)
Total	8,269		7,108	7,691	7.6%

The table above shows the planet must produce 7.6% more food in 20 years. It shows regions where demand increases and regions where demand decreases. It shows that transportation, which requires fossil fuels, will become a bigger issue. Cargo ships traversing the oceans cannot run on electric power.

There will be increased pressure for people living in areas with high fertility rates to emigrate to other areas. But is that fair?

Is it fair to the societies that mandated small families, or pressured their citizens through economic conditions to have small families, to be told that since they now have extra space, they need to open their communities to residents of other countries that chose not to control their population?

The socialist believes that it is fair to open the borders to all, but especially welcome are destitute immigrants. The socialist would make his or her point as follows: Let's assume for simplicity that society is composed of two types of "families." Family 1 has one child, family 2 has four children, and there are equal numbers of each in society. Assets are distributed equally in Generation 1, but because of family size, inherited assets are no longer equally distributed in the population. Government redistributes assets, taking from small families and giving to large families. The socialist government is popular because four out of five citizens in Generation 2 are better off financially due to redistribution.

Table 65: Example of Socialist Redistribution of Assets Based on Demographics			
	Family 1	Family 2	Total
Generation 1	2	2	4
Assets	100	100	200
Assets per Person	50	50	50
Generation 2	1	4	5
Assets	100	100	200
Assets per Person	100	25	40
Redistributed Assets	40	160	200
Redistributed Assets per Person	40	40	40

A penniless immigrant enters the socialist society, bringing the population to six. Assets must again be redistributed as illustrated below:

Table 66: Example of Socialist Redistribution of Assets with Immigration Based on Demographics				
	Family 1	Family 2	Immigrant	Total
Generation 1	2	2		4
Assets	100	100		200
Assets per Person	50	50		50
Generation 2	1	4	1	6
Assets	100	100	0	200
Assets per Person	100	25	0	33.3
Redistributed Assets	33.3	133.3	33.3	200
Redistributed Assets per Person	33.3	33.3	33.3	33.3

All Generation 2 members of society are obliged to share. The socialist leader is still popular because five out of six members of Generation 2 have a financial gain from redistribution. The Curley Effect is fully operational. The composition of society is changing in favor of those receiving net benefits. Society has started its economic decline.

Why do socialists promote open borders? Because they fundamentally do not accept property rights. They do not respect property rights, a core value for the middle class, which includes the rights of citizenship. The socialist fixation on redistributing wealth has extended to redistributing citizenship.

A country with a low fertility rate maintains reasonable employment expectations for the middle class. The supply of labor is a little tight, lifting salaries and supporting a comfortable middle-class standard of living. If this country experiences a high immigration rate, competition for jobs, downward pressure on salaries, upward pressure on housing prices, and strain on social programs would result. Also, global employment dynamics have already fundamentally changed. Many jobs can be performed remotely. An x-ray technician must be physically present, but the x-ray evaluator may reside on the other side of the globe. Many physically demanding jobs have been automated. Robots help with agriculture and street repair or mining is done with huge machines. The demand for immigrant labor, typically found in employment under harsh conditions or specialized skills, has vanished.

The citizens of countries with low fertility rates did not cause high fertility rates elsewhere. Consequently, they should not suffer adverse effects.

Actions can be taken to address high fertility rates and their consequences. World leaders at the United Nations have various asset and income redistribution systems at their disposal. Medical treatment needs to include family planning. Countries with high fertility rates are not responsible global partners. Citizens of these countries may earnestly believe that having large families is in their economic best interest. Employment or economic advancement in societies with high fertility rates must change quickly. As global citizens, they need to understand that the long-term effect of large families in today's world is disastrous. We need to avoid bumping up against the natural carrying capacity of this planet.

One action an individual country with a low fertility rate can take is to restrict the entry of any citizen from a country with a high fertility rate. No asylum seekers, workers under permit, tourists, or students would be allowed into the low fertility rate country. This would have several consequences. First, it would send a clear message that the country with the low fertility rate will not offer employment and thereby will not provide economic support to citizens of a country with a high fertility rate. Large families in countries with high fertility rates often send family members abroad to work, who then send money back to the family at home. This practice would have to cease.

Second, restricting entry for tourists and students impacts the richest 10% of a country with a high fertility rate. In most cases, only the elite of these countries have the funds to travel or educate their children abroad. Once the elite begin to experience the consequences of certain conditions, those conditions somehow change rapidly.

Third, restricting entry forces the country with a high fertility rate to feed and maintain their growing population themselves. If there are no "pressure release valves," the burgeoning population would eventually create shortages and political instability. Current leaders have a vested interest in maintaining stability.

Another action an individual country can take is to tax any money sent to countries with a high fertility rate. The tax would be imposed at the point of transmission, which is inside the originating country's borders. The tax would be imposed for any reason – purchases, gifts, or simply a transfer of funds between accounts. As the world moves to a cashless financial environment, such taxes should be feasible.

To prevent avoiding the tax by sending funds to an intermediary third country before forwarding them to a country with a high fertility rate, the fund transmission tax would also be imposed on funds sent to any other country without a cooperation agreement with the originating country or a similar taxing mechanism on high fertility rate countries.

THE MIDDLE CLASS AND CLIMATE CHANGE

In the 1940s (and it may have been earlier) an observer commented, "The government has found a way to tax everything except the air we breathe." It was a social comment made jokingly. It was a joke. Flip the pages of the calendar ahead about a hundred years. Instead of taxing the air we breathe, some politicians want to tax the air we exhale.

In 2020, global warming caused by man receives attention in the press, billions in government research grants, and is a source of public concern. The first question to ask: Why should anyone care? Observers cite a plethora of reasons but most significant is the worry that the world's ecosystems will change. As a result, decreased food production will be inadequate to feed the world.

Most people would agree that if human activities damage the environment, these activities must cease or be modified to minimize unavoidable damage.

The time horizon for a material impact of global warming is 100 years. Many changes can happen over the course of a century.

If the health of the world's ecosystems concerns us, then is global warming our most pressing problem?

What if Earth's population was only 1 billion? We know that we can raise enough food for 10 billion. Global warming may curtail food production by 20% or even 50%. In a world of 1 billion people, an adequate food supply is not an issue. Humans have survived past climate changes – warmer and cooler – and have adapted to a variety of biomes.

What if climate change did not exist? Would our ecosystems still be threatened? We have already seen that with current fertility rates, global food production must increase in the next 20 years. Over the next 100 years, global food production must steadily increase to a level of about five times the current production. Sub-Saharan Africa would be by far the largest consumer of food due to the large number of children produced generation after generation.

The following table projects the food consumed for the next century, assuming no changes in fertility rates or the mix of food between animal, vegetable, and processed.

Table 67: Estimated Food Requirements for the Next 100 Years – Environmental Impact

		Food Consumed					
Region	Growth in Food Consumption Every 20 Years	Currently	In 20 Years	In 40 Years	In 60 Years	In 80 Years	In 100 Years
East Asia	(9.8%)	2,098	1,892	1,706	1,539	1,388	1,251
India	6.5%	526	560	596	635	676	719
N Africa and Mid East	27.4%	771	982	1,251	1,593	2,029	2,584
Sub-Sahara Africa	115.1%	670	1,441	3,099	6,666	14,336	30,833
S America	1.0%	712	719	726	733	740	748
Europe	(15.2%)	1,145	971	823	698	592	502
US & Canada	(4.2%)	873	836	801	767	734	703
Russia	(6.7%)	224	209	195	182	170	158
Australia	(9.0%)	89	81	74	67	61	56
Total		7,108	7,691	9,271	12,880	20,726	37,554

	Food Consumed					
	Currently	In 20 Years	In 40 Years	In 60 Years	In 80 Years	In 100 Years
Total	7,108	7,691	9,271	12,880	20,726	37,554
Increase Over Current	0	583	2,163	5,772	13,618	30,446
Percentage Increase Over Current		8.2%	30.4%	81.2%	191.6%	428.3%

The impact on the planet's ecosystems will be enormous – far greater than any effects of climate change. We will begin to see damage from high fertility rates to our ecosystems in 20 to 40 years, much sooner than climate change's time horizon.

For each square kilometer (or acre) currently used for agriculture, we must convert another four square kilometers of pristine land into farmland. We must increase current agricultural and livestock yields per square kilometer, requiring fertilizer, chemicals, antibiotics, hormones, and pesticides. These chemicals will pollute cities as well as forests and wetlands.

The oceans would have to produce five times as much fish or other seafood, a highly unlikely scenario. Finally, one of the most overlooked crises is the decline of the bee population. Already under threat of extinction by pesticides, bees will have no uncontaminated havens in the future, which will mean fruit and vegetable crop failures.

Most would agree that if human activities damage the environment, then these activities must cease entirely or be modified to minimize their harmful effects. Overpopulation is hurting the environment. The damage will worsen over time if not effectively addressed. Humans may not have complete control over climate change. The sun undergoes periods of relative solar activity and hibernation. We have historical evidence of warmer and cooler periods that could not possibly have been caused by mankind. Overpopulation, on the other hand, is entirely under human control. The sooner we bring fertility rates down, the less permanent damage we do to our ecosystems, and the lower the risks will be of an inadequate food supply.

The Paris Agreement of the United Nations of 2016 was aimed at reducing carbon dioxide emissions. This is a noble goal. Research and development of alternative energy offer meaningful employment to the middle class. But the Paris Agreement had questionable provisions. One such provision was to take funds from developed countries and give them to underdeveloped countries, ostensibly to help them reduce their carbon emissions. If these funds are earmarked for research and engineering, why export this money and the jobs it would create?

The Paris Agreement did not address population levels or growth. One simple way to reduce man's carbon dioxide emissions by 20% is to reduce the number of people by 20%. This can be done by lowering fertility rates.

Evidently, the redistribution mentality has taken precedence over a mentality promoting economic growth. The Paris Agreement undertook no study or consideration of the effectiveness or rate of return of funds invested in improving carbon dioxide emissions. Government waste effectively takes resources away from the middle class.

And now, since carbon dioxide is officially a pollutant, governments need to impose some kind of tax. Chickens pollute and cows pollute but most importantly, people pollute every time they exhale. The middle class needs to be very careful about who they elect to government.

THE MIDDLE CLASS AND NUCLEAR WEAPONS

The subject of mutual annihilation is not discussed much anymore. It should be a concern because of the importance of who has his or her finger on the nuclear trigger.

Who would you rather have making the decision to launch nuclear weapons – someone who truly believes in God or someone who believes in might makes right? Even if you personally do not believe in God, you have to reluctantly admit that the world is in better hands when those hands are praying.

A moral compass on both sides of a disagreement will prevent escalation into war. Wars have been fought for many reasons. Access to resources. Redress.

Escalation can sometimes be avoided if one attempts to understand the "enemy." There may be no appeasing the other side and war may be the final way to settle serious differences. One of the parties cannot keep retreating and retreating in response to hostile threats.

Who would make the better negotiator - someone who truly believes in God or someone who believes in might makes right? A negotiator with no moral compass has no credibility with an opposing party. People know when attempts are being made to manipulate them. People recognize deceit, intimidation, force, coercion, and subversion. They respond with mistrust and guarded inaction at best and with similar conduct at worst. Thus, conflicts elude resolution and disputes fester.

A moral negotiator with religious convictions has a great deal of credibility. A moral negotiator presents and discusses issues fully and honestly. A moral leader has boundaries that the opposing leader understands and respects. "Enemies" may not like each other, but if they have mutual respect, then conflicts can potentially be resolved. A wise leader knows that he or she may possibly be wrong. A wise leader knows that both parties must somehow win.

A civil society needs leaders – political and military – with religious training and a religious commitment. These are the people who hold the fate of billions in their hands. The middle class has much to gain by electing a leader who commands respect, and much to lose by electing someone who simply panders to the masses.

AN ANALOGY

From the dawn of human existence, people believed that Earth was the center of the universe. As early as 300 BC, some ancient Greeks proposed that the Sun, not the Earth, was actually the universe's center. Geocentrism is the doctrine that puts the Earth at the center while heliocentrism maintains that the Sun is the center of the universe.

Geocentrists had some valid points. First, from the time of their birth they were told the Earth was the center of the universe. Everyone knew that! Second, it was impossible for the Earth to spin and circle the Sun. We would feel the motion. The wind would blow constantly and objects would fall slightly sideways.

In the 1500s, astronomer Nicholas Copernicus wrote a book containing his celestial measurements and why these measurements were consistent with a heliocentric universe. Specifically, a heliocentric model explained the retrograde motion of the planets. The model also put the stars' distances from the Earth orders of magnitude farther than the planets' distances. It took a long time for the scientific community to accept the heliocentric model, and not until around 1700 did it become widely accepted as reality.

The notion of heliocentrism was not readily embraced. The Greeks proposed it 2,000 years before it became accepted. People believed in a system taught to them, in a system their parents and peers unquestioningly thought was true. Even though scientific evidence pointed to a heliocentric system, many people at the time could not bring themselves accept such an idea.

Communism and Socialism have been economic and political systems of beliefs since the 1850s. Like the geocentric model, schools and parents have taught children that socialism works, and if implemented correctly, can lead to a better, more equitable life for all. Many teachers touting socialism have not even considered viewing it as a mere belief system – one without an actual working model.

As in the case of heliocentrism, scientific evidence to the contrary has been accumulating. The academic community and the public just need to look. With the Internet, the evidence is readily available. However, wisdom is required to process this information.

The purpose of this *Middle Class Manifesto* is to make the world a better and more equitable place. Some of the manifesto's sections are quite detailed, and apologies are given to readers who find these boring. Sometimes copious detail is needed to convey new ideas.

This manifesto was created outside of academia and without any political sponsorship. Like Copernicus' book, numerical data and examples are given to support the various recommendations. Many recommendations have yet to be tried because they represent a departure from the status quo or simply have not been proposed before now. This effort was worthwhile if it sparks interest in further exploration. There is quite a bit of economic, behavioral, historical, and theological material available. Effective research can lead to intelligent discussion and ultimately to actions that will improve society.

I sincerely hope the reader is a better person for having read this manifesto. Please share it. Thank you for reading.

Made in United States
Troutdale, OR
11/03/2026

56845390R00099